D1615022

From Calais to Colditz

From Calais to Colditz

A Rifleman's Memoir
of Captivity and Escape

Philip Pardoe

Pen & Sword
MILITARY

First published in Great Britain in 2016 by
PEN & SWORD MILITARY
an imprint of
Pen & Sword Books Ltd
47 Church Street
Barnsley
South Yorkshire, S70 2AS

ISBN 978 1 47387 539 5

Printed and bound in England by
CPI Group (UK) Ltd, Croydon, CR0 4YY

Typeset in Times by CHIC GRAPHICS

Pen & Sword Books Ltd incorporates the imprints of Aviation, Atlas,
Family History, Fiction, Maritime, Military, Discovery, Politics, History,
Archaeology, Select, Wharncliffe Local History, Wharncliffe True Crime,
Military Classics, Wharncliffe Transport, Leo Cooper, The Praetorian
Press, Remember When, Seaforth Publishing and Frontline Publishing.

For a complete list of Pen & Sword titles please contact
PEN & SWORD BOOKS LIMITED
47 Church Street, Barnsley, South Yorkshire, S70 2AS, England
E-mail: enquiries@pen-and-sword.co.uk
Website: www.pen-and-sword.co.uk

Contents

Foreword

During some five years as a prisoner-of-war I recorded, largely in the form of notes, my recollections of the Battle of Calais and of my subsequent experiences in seven different camps. Two years after my release, while commanding a company in Palestine, I recorded these memoirs in the form of a consecutive narrative. I was on active service at the time and greatly helped by my company clerk, Lance Corporal Jenner, who typed them out in his spare time. The original notes were sketchy and of necessity omitted anything that could have been of interest to the Germans. The subsequent narrative was intended to fill in as many gaps as possible but my primary motive was the interest of my family and a few very close friends and for forty years I forgot all about them.

In 1985 I unearthed the only surviving copy and, after reading it, I began to wonder whether it might be of interest to a wider public. I was tempted to re-write much of it, partly to fill in more detail on such events as the great escape over the wire from Warburg, and partly to change the rather naïve style of the narrative. But I decided that part of its interest could be in leaving it very much as it was written at the time with a few adjustments to assist in identifying some of the personalities and put some of the events in a more intelligible context.

I dedicate this memoir to Martin Gilliat who was like an elder brother to me during those years and hope that a few members of my family and of my regiment will find something of interest in these pages in years to come.

P.P.

Acknowledgements

I am so pleased that my late father's war memoirs are being published. It has been a concern to me to think that this record of his war experiences might be lost, as it was originally put on very thin paper and several copies were mislaid. It is reassuring to know that my children, family and relations and, of course, the Regiment will be able to read what is a remarkable account in a better format.

He was a wonderful father to my sister, Caroline and myself and devoted husband to our mother, Rolline. He was a very supportive, funny, kind and modest man and a true gentleman who always seemed to have all the time for everyone.

Like my late Godfather, Martin Gilliat, who features in this story, my father rarely, if ever, discussed the war. How fortunate that he committed his memoirs to paper.

I would like to thank Jon Cooksey for his permission to use photographs and maps from his book *Calais – A Fight to the Finish*.

I am very grateful to John Jay for allowing me the use of material and maps from *Facing Fearful Odds,* his account of his own father's experiences at Calais and as a PoW.

I am also indebted to Valentine West for generously offering the use of his father's artwork. Our fathers were PoWs together at Laufen in late 1940.

Finally I thank everyone at Pen and Sword Books Ltd, especially Henry Wilson, Christopher Robinson, Matt Jones and Jon Wilkinson. Without their support this book would not have been possible.

Harry Pardoe
2016

Chapter 1

Before Calais

No-one who paid a casual visit to the 2nd Battalion, King's Royal Rifle Corps, billeted in Dorset in the spring of 1940, would have noticed any undue activity or preparations for going into motion. The Blitzkrieg had burst upon France in April and German divisions, having broken through, were pouring toward the Channel coast; the Battalion, however, seemed as far away from the war as in Tidworth days and not an enemy bomber disturbed the routine of our weekly training programmes.

I had joined the Battalion from Chisledon early in March and was posted to Number 9 Platoon, the Scout Platoon of 'C' Company. Maurice Johnson was commanding the Company into which he had infused a remarkably cheerful spirit. Although gruff outwardly to men and officers alike, he was much respected and liked by the men if a little too insensible to the comfort and feelings of some of his officers for their full approval.

Everard Radcliffe, his second-in-command, was an excellent counter-balancing influence. He was exceptionally gifted and artistic, loathed discomfort and had the happy knack of getting his own way. He was the only married one of us and lived in Shillingstone. The other platoon commanders – Peter Parker, Pat Sherrard and I – lived with Maurice in a comfortable cottage in Child Okeford, where the Company was billeted.

We spent those lovely spring days training either by platoons or as a company and on two or three occasions we had battalion exercises. Few men knew their weapons really well, owing to lack of firing practice, and battle drill was a word as yet unknown but none of us doubted that we were one of the best trained battalions in the army and quite a match for anything the Germans might have.

One evening, after dining well, we had just gone up to bed when a rifleman arrived on his motor bike with a message for Maurice. We gathered in the dining room – Sergeant Major Childs had also appeared from somewhere – and heard the news. The Battalion was to be ready to move with war loads by midnight. It seemed probable that this was the preparatory move before embarkation. It was what we had been anticipating since 3 September.

We all felt slightly dramatic. Most of us felt that this period of make-believe was over and that this was the real thing. We pretended to be even more pleased than we were in our fear of appearing unenthusiastic for action. We passed the port hurriedly round and then I got into my car to visit Everard.

Nobody appeared to be at home in his cottage and, as I was groping round in the darkness of the hall, he and Betty came in the front door after an evening stroll. I broke the news to them breathlessly and with little tact. Everard made no attempt to disguise his feelings of dread. For him the sword of Damocles had at last fallen and he and Betty were to be parted.

I hurried back, told my servant to pack my things and went down to the Company Office. Loading carriers in pitch darkness was far from easy. Bren guns, Boys rifles, rifles, tripods, ammunition, Verey light pistols, aiming lamps, hand grenades, camouflage nets, ration tins, water cans, tools, maps, concertina wire, tarpaulin, anti-gas equipment – all had their allotted place. We had practised loading and everyone knew his job and, by 2330 hours, all my carriers were ready to move. Only my Sergeant Dryborough-Smith and one or two men who had been to a dance in Sturminster Newton were late. Dryborough-Smith was a big tall fair-haired regular with much service in a chequered career. He had been to a public school and went to Sandhurst as an 'A' cadet but got sent down and was usually 'on the provost'. He had a bit of the bully in him and was not liked, if much feared, by the men. Our relations were strained but superficially good. I respected his efficiency while disliking his methods and we avoided quarrelling. That night I suspected him of being deliberately late but said nothing.

The news of the move had spread through the village like wildfire. The riflemen had endeared themselves to the local inhabitants in an extraordinary way and, now that we were leaving, the girls came to say goodbye to their boyfriends and there was much sobbing and kissing. Once the order arrived we were soon ready to leave next morning at 0630 hours. We went to bed and snatched a hurried sleep. I woke early, bundled all my belongings which I did not want to take into my car, drove to the Glazebrooks' house and scribbled two notes – one to her and one to my family.

We left Child Okeford punctually The Battalion moved in two columns, one for wheeled and one for tracked vehicles. Mike Sinclair commanded the latter. We received our route to Ware [near Hertford] via Salisbury, Newbury and Reading.

Despite the early hour the whole village was up to wave goodbye – with many in tears. As we were passing through Shillingstone, I saw Betty standing alone looking miserably unhappy. She had just said goodbye to Norman [Philips] for the last time. I waved to her but she never saw me. I felt sad as I realised what our parting meant to others and yet elated at the thought of the adventure that lay ahead. The wind blew fresh in our faces and the dew was still on the grass. It was good to be doing something at last.

The drive was uneventful. About mid-day we halted near Newbury, opposite an aerodrome, to fill up with petrol. Something had gone wrong with the ration truck which had not yet appeared so we bought some meat pies and sausages from a canteen nearby. A string of traffic passed us – race-goers on their way to the Spring Cup. Wonderful memories flashed through my mind and made me sad for a while.

We moved on again and in every town crowds thronging the streets waved to us as we crashed through. They were giving us a great send-off. To them we were the reassuring answer to the bad news from France. We waved back proudly at first but soon grew weary of this.

By the time we approached Hertford it was getting dark. We were tired and hungry. Apart from two punctures to my motor bikes all had hitherto gone well but here I found one carrier was missing. It caught me up after a few minutes and I learnt that the exhaust pipe had set the camouflage net on fire but little damage was done.

A guide led us in pitch darkness to our billet in Ware which was very bad – an old disused house with no lights or water, many floor boards broken and strewn with shattered glass from the windows. We were all tired and bad tempered and consequently a bit snappish. I was very glad to get into my flea-bag for the night. We were up early next morning and, after gathering my platoon and telling them to see to the maintenance of their vehicles and weapons, Maurice and I left for a tactical reconnaissance near Rayleigh. The Company were to join us there later in the day.

We were told that the Germans were expected to attempt a landing on the coast at any time and perhaps to drop parachutists. We were to reconnoitre all roads in the district which led to likely vulnerable points and liaise with the Pioneer Corps who had prepared a number of road blocks.

The Company arrived about tea time and was billeted in a girls' school with both officers and men sleeping on the floor in different rooms. The officers of all other companies were billeted centrally and feeding and living very much more comfortably; I felt this was a great injustice.

The next few days were spent with our NCOs reconnoitring the road blocks and vulnerable points in our area. I celebrated my 21st birthday by being called at midnight and told to stand by from 0200 hours onwards, as the Germans were expected that morning. Visions of scoring 'first blood' that day were disappointed. It was one of many false alarms. During the day I got several letters and birthday presents, including a gold compass from Mum, a photo from Flick, and a dry fly line from Dad which I sent straight home! The fishing prospects did not look good. Best of all a large box of chocolates arrived from Fortnums which we quickly dealt with.

The next day we were once more on the move – a short drive this time through Bury St Edmunds to Fornham Park. Apart from one of my carriers knocking over a telegraph pole there were no mishaps on the way. Fornham Park was a distinct improvement with a large house, in which some sapper officers were billeted, and lovely grounds which must have provided a good pheasant shoot. With the Battalion I slept under canvas in ideal weather to the sound of the nightingales singing in my ears.

The officers messed together in a marquee and for me this was the first time we had all been together during the war. By day we reconnoitred the roads in the Harwich areas – a raid was expected on the port. We were at very short notice to move and had little chance to get away. One evening, after a hot and tiring day, we were asked to go over to a private school next door to bathe in their swimming bath. It was wonderfully refreshing. The washing question was difficult. I used an old woman's house in Rayleigh, but the men were very short of water until a diviner arrived and sank an artesian well which threatened to flood the area.

One day Martin, Peter Parker and I decided we needed a really good dinner. We would go into Bury and order roast duck, Bollinger '28, etc. And we persuaded the Colonel, Euan Miller, to try to get us permission to go to Newmarket races next day. We drove into the town and went first to the hairdresser. As we emerged licking our chops at the thought of our dinner, the Provost Corporal drew up on his motor cycle: 'All ranks return to camp at once.'

We managed to secure a taxi and on the way back picked up a number of riflemen including Sergeant Dryborough-Smith. The camp was seething with activity – tents being struck, vehicles loaded in record time and even Tucker was busy packing my valise. I changed from Service Dress into Battle Dress putting on plenty of warm clothing. My platoon was present and ready to move by 2000 hours.

At dinner I heard that we were to move at 2330 hours. Everyone was in a state of suppressed excitement. Humour had it that this was no invasion scare – it was the real thing. After dinner Tony Turner came round to see me. He was in tears and very agitated. He managed to stammer out that Tony Stallard, the MO, had forbidden him to come with us as he suspected a mastoid in his ear. Tony has been to see Godfrey Cromwell and the Colonel and caused a dreadful scene but both were adamant. He swore it was the worst blow fate had ever dealt him. I was very sad and tried to comfort him by saying he would probably join us in a week. He left me in tears.

All was now ready but there were still two hours to go. The Company sat round in a circle and sang all the old favourites. It was a lovely night. Just before 2300 hours we started up the carriers and moved to the forming up position at the Park gates. Maps were issued and the route given – Newmarket, London, Winchester, Southampton. Our doubts were finally dispelled. It was France at last.

First the wheeled vehicles, then the carriers moved off – 20 yards between vehicles and 200 yards between sections. The DR [Despatch Rider] of each section kept in touch with the section in front and did 'traffic control'. With dimmed lights progress was slow and it seemed a long time before we reached Newmarket, 20 miles off. I recalled the last time I was there, when Norman, Bill Fyfe and I flew up from Tidworth for the 'Guineas'.

Every two hours the column halted. On the first such occasion an order came back that all lights were to be extinguished. It was intended to refer only to the actual period of the halt but this was not made clear. So instead of being guided by a long string of tail lights, like a luminous string of beads, we could only see ten yards ahead. This was very dangerous for the DRs. By 0330 hours I was feeling tired. The road appeared straight forward so I dozed off to sleep. I woke up some time later to find we had stopped in a country lane. My 10 carriers were drawn up behind but there was no sign of the column.

My DR, Perry, thinking he saw the next carrier turn off, had led my whole platoon up a side road and had just realised his mistake. I heard the noise of some carriers approaching and next minute a whole section swept round the corner straight towards us. Perry was standing in the middle of the road with no lights on and only just got out of the way in time. I flashed my torch and they pulled up having made the same mistake as us.

We all hustled back to the main road, where we joined the Brigade HQ Group, whom we passed and at the next halt regained our position in the column. As I was trying to sort out the muddle I was hailed in broad Lancashire and there was Smith, Grismond Davies-Scourfield's servant, who had looked after us at Blandford Camp. I had not seen him since and we were both very pleased to meet. He was a great character and I was very fond of him.

We continued the journey. I changed my drivers and alternately drove a carrier, a motor bike and slept. We were short of reserve DRs and Filkins had to drive the whole way unrelieved – a great feat. Passing through London it started to rain. I was on a motor bike at the time luckily wearing my mackintosh but everything and everyone got soaked. We filled up with petrol in London and stopped for breakfast on Hertford Bridge flats about 1030 hours. We were just by Roberts' gallops where I used to train Grecian Isle for the Sandhurst point-to-point. The rain stopped and we soon dried out as we rattled along that Tidworth-London road I knew so well.

By the time we were approaching Southampton the DRs were very exhausted. Perry went to sleep and drove into the ditch – luckily without doing any damage. Moffat, the Battalion Motor Transport [MT] Sergeant, did the same and had to be taken to hospital with a cut knee. That was the only bad accident on the whole journey. In Southampton some immaculate Staff Officers relieved us of our maps and some kind people gave us hot tea and buns which were very welcome. The drivers took the vehicles off to be loaded while the remainder of the Battalion was directed to a rest camp for a wash and a hot meal.

John Christian and Mac McClure were waiting there. They had come over from the depot to see us off. It was good to see John again after so long. Together with Martin Gilliat [later Lieutenant Colonel Sir Martin Gilliat, GCVO, MBE] and Norman we went off to have tea in a café. There we bought plenty of chocolate and ate a proper hunting tea of scrambled eggs and bacon. Norman rang up Aunt Margaret to say goodbye. I wondered whether to do the same but decided it would be too painful. So I sent off a wire saying 'Cook the ducks to-night'. It was a prearranged code which Dad had used in the last war, for exactly the same purpose, before embarking for France.

We returned to the camp and the Battalion formed up wearing full equipment to march through the town to the boat. It was a moving experience. Crowds on the pavement cheered as we went by and here and there a handkerchief was raised to damp eyes. These people, mostly women, saw war stripped of its glamour and knew from experience the tragedy it entailed. Some had sons or husbands in the Battalion and were wondering how many would return.

But to these people I scarcely gave a thought. I was filled with pride and gratitude that I was going into action with the Battalion I loved, just as my father had done in the last war. Here at last was an opportunity to pay back something that I owed to my regiment and country. We passed a field where a cricket match was in progress. Few of the players bothered to give us a glance. But, far from resenting this, I felt sorry for them that they had not a similar opportunity and so could not share my feelings. A number of riflemen from the depot, mostly old and unfit, kept pace with us, chatting and joking. 'Good luck, mate, wish I were in your boots.' They really meant it.

At the docks the roll was called and the Battalion reported present. In single files we trooped on board. There were three ships waiting – one for us, one for the Rifle Brigade who had come down from Essex and one for our transport. The other two regiments forming our brigade – the Queen Victoria Rifles [QVRs] and the 1ˢᵗ Tank Regiment – had left the day before and were already across the Channel. Our weapons were stacked on deck and Maurice told me to post a sentry on them. It was only just in time, for in a few minutes I met Norman who had lost a Bren gun somehow. I felt very smug. All Ranks were then assembled with lifebelts strapped on and we were told where to go on the 'Alarm' or 'Abandon Ship'. I visited my platoon in their quarters below. They were very cramped but no-one seemed to mind the discomfort.

Most of the officers bedded down in the smoking room but a few had cabins. I thought I had discovered an unoccupied one until Puffin [Major O.S. Owen] arrived and turned me out. Tucker as usual had disappeared. He was a young militiaman whom I had only known a few weeks. He was obviously unsuitable as a servant, but in the recent busy days, I had found no time to select another from the DRs. At last I got my things together and went into the dining room. We had a first class meal with two double whiskies costing only half a crown. I turned in early with the rest under way for Dover.

Called at 0400 hours I dressed hurriedly, not knowing where we should find ourselves, and once on deck recognised the famous white cliffs. We were lying just off the harbour. I was Orderly Officer and, having seen tea issued to each company, inspected the Anti-Aircraft Posts. One had no tracer ammunition and another only two magazines which would have lasted half a minute.

Down below breakfast was being served – the last proper meal for several weeks and the last eggs and bacon for years. But we never gave this possibility a thought. Presently the boat put into Dover harbour and a number of people sent off letters to their homes. Unfortunately I never thought of this until too late. In higher circles great decisions were being taken and the Brigadier, Claude Nicholson, was receiving his final orders from the War Office.

About mid-day we got under way aboard *SS Royal Daffodil* for Calais. The three transports were escorted by four destroyers, zig zagging in front and on both flanks. Overhead the odd fighter roared past but there were not as many as I had expected. The sea was flat calm.

We were just getting down to a meal of cold bully beef and biscuits when suddenly the alarm rung out. All ranks crowded down below deck where we were packed tight as sardines. I looked round and thought of the massacre if a bomb landed in their midst. As if to confirm my thoughts, an explosion shook the whole ship, followed by a rattle, and our Anti-Aircraft guns went into action. One could distinguish between them and the louder reports of the destroyers' heavier guns. We could only guess what was happening but I heard later that a German bomber, flying high, had dropped two bombs between our boat and that of the Rifle Brigade before making off in safety.

There followed a long wait broken by the sound of another explosion. This time depth charges had been dropped as submarines were suspected in the neighbourhood. It was distinctly unpleasant down below.

Presently Maurice appeared, having come straight from a company commanders' conference. Everard, Pat Sherrard, Peter, PSM Simpson and I collected for orders. He issued maps of the Calais area and explained the general situation. The Germans had broken through and light armoured units were believed to be approaching Calais. These were said to consist of motor cyclists and possibly a few tanks. Our task was to attack their lines of communication. 'C' Company was to disembark last and proceed on foot to an assembly area out on the sand dunes to await the transport. On the arrival of the trucks and carriers, the Company was to move to Guines. The enemy were said to have air superiority and would probably machine gun and bomb us as we disembarked.

The news was far worse than I had expected. During the last few days none of us had followed events in France very closely. I had heard Churchill's speech describing the 'Battle of the Bulge', and Duff Cooper's speech had surprised me when he said that even if France were lost the war would go on. How could France be defeated? She had the best army in the world and a great counter-attack would certainly restore the situation.

Perhaps the Germans had fallen into the very trap the French had laid for them. And this business about a few motor cyclists near

Calais – why? The Channel ports had held out in the last war against the whole might of the German army for four years. How could they fall in as many weeks?

Unconvinced in my own mind, I saw my section commanders and passed on the information. They asked me questions such as 'How can we tell a German tank from an English one?' I had no idea. I didn't even know what uniform they wore. I was ashamed of my ignorance and reproached myself for not finding out these fundamental and essential details in the past months. What hours had been wasted on training and learning 'military vocabulary fire orders' and such-like. Our unpreparedness for war began to dawn upon me.

Chapter 2

The First Day – 23 May

One after the other the ships steamed into Calais and the disembarkation began. Impatiently 'C' Company waited for the rest of the Battalion but no bombers came over. Standing on deck I thought I recognised one of the ratings. He came up to me and I saw it was a friend of mine at Eton called Marriott. He told me he had enlisted as a signaller but we had little time to talk for soon it was our turn to leave.

The last man was safely ashore and we felt distinctly happier on dry land. Rifles and revolvers were loaded and we filed through the town northward to the sand dunes. There were frequent halts to let those in front get on. I noticed one or two houses burning and asked a French workman what had been happening. He said the bombers were over early that morning and three were shot down. Shortly afterwards the air raid siren sounded.

Once away from the town the Battalion strung out along a narrow causeway – a canal on the right and a lake known as the Basin de Chasses on the left. Here and there a fresh shell hole showed that other troops, taking the same path, had not been so lucky. We all wore full equipment, carrying our great coats. A heavy drizzle started to fall and we let down our gas capes. They made very good waterproofs. At last we reached the assembly area and could take off our heavy packs.

We took up a position in scrubby country facing east. A broad sandy strip separated 'B' and 'C' Companies. Sergeant Dryborough-Smith's section faced North West and Sergeant Crowther's North East. Crowther was a reservist whom I like very much. Although a bit vague, he had a good section and got on well with everyone. I had great hopes of him. I put Sergeant Colotta's section in reserve. He was a dark and slightly foreign looking reservist who lacked imagination but was otherwise efficient.

Having visited each section, I crossed over to 'B' Company's area to arrange with Dick Scott for cross-fire between our platoons, to deal with some dead ground to the north. I then felt quite happy about our all-round protection. The rain fell steadily and now and then, somewhere away to the east, the rattle of machine-guns kept us on the alert.

After an hour and a half I was summoned to Maurice's headquarters. He gave us the startling news that German advanced units were much nearer than expected and tanks were even rumoured to be in the streets of Calais. He ordered two motor platoons and my Scout platoon to block certain roads leading eastwards out of Calais, while one motor platoon remained in reserve at Fort Risban. I pointed out to him that my eleven Bren Guns and Boys Rifles were still with the Carriers on the boat and that my total armament was twelve revolvers and twenty rifles, which would be useless against a tank. He saw my point at once and ordered my platoon into reserve.

We marched back to Calais by the same way that we had left. The rain had stopped but our coats and packs felt very heavy. Intermittently there sounded a burst of machine-gun fire perhaps 3 or 4 miles away. My map showed no way of crossing the docks except by marching three quarters of the way round the town. This we did and only later did I find that we could have crossed a bridge in a straight line with Fort Risban. The maps were very inaccurate.

As we approached the fort a machine gun opened up from a top window behind our backs and bullets ricocheted past. My platoon was moving on either side of the street well dispersed and no-one was hit. Like lightning every man was in a doorway or cellar, peering up at the houses, but there was nothing to be seen. I put it down to an excitable Frenchman who had mistaken us for the Germans or a Fifth Columnist. It would take too long to search every house so I carried on.

Shortly after, I heard a babble of voices behind and looked round to see a car coming towards me pursued by an angry crowd of civilians. The car drew up beside me and to my amazement out stepped Maurice. Instantly we were surrounded by a swarm of excited Frenchmen shouting and gesticulating. Out of the babble of voices, I distinguished the words *'espion'* and *'arretes'*. Maurice, who could not understand a word of French, told me he had just commandeered the car.

After a time, I managed to make myself heard and explained to the crowd that this was not a spy but my Company commander. Convinced at last they went off on another line. A time bomb had been placed in the car and would blow up any moment. They implored Maurice not to get into it. This was too much for him and, after giving me my orders, he drove off and the crowd dispersed muttering to themselves. They evidently resented his method of commandeering.

This was my first experience of the French en masse. I was astounded at their hysterical behaviour. No rumour seemed too improbable for them. I gathered that parachutists in civilian clothes had recently been dropped by the Germans and were suspected to be mingling with them. This had put their nerves more on edge than usual.

I now took up a position by Fort Risban, on the high ground overlooking a moat and railway. Dryborough-Smith watched the Calais Bridge, Crowther the Sangatte road and Coletta in reserve posted sentries in the rear. Air sentries were put out by each section to watch especially for parachutists. I was there about an hour before I discovered two men with an anti-tank rifle so sited that, if fired, it could hardly fail to hit one of my platoon. They appeared to belong to an Anti-Tank Company but where they came from I could not make out; I moved them so that they covered the bridge.

Several hours passed and nothing happened. The platoon had taken off their packs and were eating haversack rations when an enemy aeroplane flew high over us, leaving a long trail of smoke in the air. AA guns on the fort opened fire and tracer bullets could be seen flying after the plane. British fighters appeared and drove it off.

Shortly after there was a swish and a bang as half a dozen shells landed in the moat forty yards ahead. Nothing indicated where they came from or whether they were directed against us or the bridge. We froze to the ground and splinters flew low over our heads or thudded into the turf, one of them very near Sergeant Floater. This was our 'baptism of fire', and had a stimulating effect. No-one had known how he would react but now we felt a new confidence in ourselves. The shells probably came from long range artillery with whom the aeroplane was in contact leaving its smoke trail as an aiming mark.

No more shells came over but German aeroplanes appeared from time to time. They were at once engaged with AA fire and driven off by our fighters who appeared to have local air superiority. We never saw a plane shot down but there was a spectacular duel right over our heads – one plane chasing the other which swerved, dived and performed every manoeuvre before disappearing from sight

Just as dusk was coming on some trucks and carriers which, from the yellow triangle on their sides, we recognised as ours emerged from the docks and drove into a large goods yard beyond the railway. This yard, which measured about 300 by 100 yards, had a metal surface and was chosen for 'C' Company's harbour. All vehicles as they arrived were dispersed around it as far apart as possible and concealed from the air by camouflage netting. My platoon was then called in and tasked to block all roads leading into the goods yard.

There were about a thousand large barrels of Epernay red wine stacked in the yard. These we laboriously rolled into all the gaps. They were very heavy and each one required about 5 men to roll it up hill. By the time we had finished it was pitch dark.

The enemy now started regular shelling of the town and, although most seemed to be falling some way off, a number of rifle shots were going off uncomfortably close. Undoubtedly some of these came from Fifth Columnists but the majority from the French troops to whom every figure in the dark was a potential enemy.

Colour Sergeant Frost lost no time in starting up the company cooker and soon we were all enjoying a hot meal and a strong brew of tea. My day's work was far from done as my platoon had to find guards for the two main entrances to the yard as well as the bridge. I ran into a Belgian officer who had been chauffeuring Maurice during the day and gave him a meal. He was an amusing person and told me he had captained the Belgian hockey team against England last year. We were soon firm friends. He said the whole of his regiment had been wiped out in Belgium and he alone had managed to escape. He had a very fine car which he lent me to stiffen up one of my road blocks. I saw nothing odd in his story at the time and, for all I know, it may have been true.

About 1100 the shells seemed to be falling much closer. We were in a particularly vulnerable position from shell splinters flying off the metal surface and so, acting on instructions from Battalion HQ, Maurice moved the whole Company less my platoon along the Sangatte road to a point on the sand dunes just clear of the town. I was to stay behind and keep guard on the road blocks.

The Company moved out without lights and disappeared into the night and I was left alone. I visited my sentry posts. As they all seemed well sited and quite happy I got into my carrier for a bit of sleep. My Belgian friend decided to stay with me and got into his car which was helping to block a road, covered by Anti-Tank Rifles, etc. Heaven help him if a tank had come along.

I had not been asleep more than a few minutes before I was woken by Lance Corporal Greenaway, one of Maurice's DRs. He was very excited and short of breath. The gist of his message was that an intercepted German wireless report stated that the goods yard and bridge were to be blown up within a few minutes. We were to pack up at once and he would lead us to join the rest of the Company.

It all sounded highly improbable but the shelling was certainly getting nearer and I was glad of any excuse to leave the goods yard. Road blocks were quickly cleared, carriers started up and a close column [including the Belgian officer's car] was formed and prepared to move. Greenaway started off at about 50 mph leaving me well behind but soon recovered his head and came back leading us at a more reasonable pace.

It was a relief to see my last carrier clear of the bridge and to be heading for more open country. The sniping and shelling had been an unnerving experience and outside the town things seemed much healthier. After arriving safely at the new Company harbour I was met by Maurice who showed me where to park my carriers. He also told me to block the road into Calais. I posted Crowther's section on the road and, dog-tired, climbed into my carrier, covered myself with a blanket and was soon fast asleep.

Chapter 3

The Second Day – 24 May

About two hours later I was woken by Maurice. He told me to take out a patrol at dawn to reconnoitre to the south, leaving at 0530 hours. His instructions were very vague and I was still half asleep. I warned Dryborough-Smith's section to be ready and, telling one of the sentries to call me at 0515 hours, went back to my carrier for some more sleep.

I was called punctually and gave my patrol their orders. We would go as far as Sangatte and, turning left in the village, return to Calais via Coquelles. Everard got up especially to see me off and checked my route. He said it would take too long and that we must return the same way as we went out. This alteration almost certainly had very important consequences.

The French had laid land mines on the right of the road so I told all carriers to keep well to the left. I travelled in the second one, with Dryborough-Smith's and another behind me. As we went along I chalked in on my big talc map case the positions of French posts and some gunners up on the cliffs to the right and of the QVRs in Sangatte.

Having reached the far side of this village Lance Corporal Brown in the leading carrier turned round and we started back. Soon I heard the noise of machine-gun fire from the direction of the Coquelles Road. I could not tell whether it was coming from the enemy or our own troops but marked on my map the approximate position whence it seemed to come. A little further on I saw some yellow Verey lights going up to the right. They looked suspicious and I decided to investigate. I signalled to Brown and we went down a rough lane, searching the area fairly carefully, but saw no sign of friend or foe. I noted the position and we carried on back. Passing the cliffs, we saw that the gunners were firing rapidly in the direction whence I had heard the machine-gun fire.

I arrived back at 0630 hours and was met by Maurice who was waiting impatiently. He said he had expected me back earlier and why had I sent back no wireless message? Our orders were not to use the wireless except for important messages and I had not considered that I had any to give and told him so. I reported what I had seen and gave him my map case, while he radioed my report through to Battalion HQ.

I learnt later that Dick Scott had also taken a patrol out that morning. Along the Coquelles Road he ran into some German posts which knocked out all his carriers but one. Dick decided at once to attack on foot. He suffered fairly heavy casualties and was himself wounded in the ankle. Few of his patrol got back, but one rifleman described how single-handed Dick attacked and wiped out a machine-gun post before making his way painfully back across country.

This was the machine-gun fire that I had heard and, had I kept to my original route returning to Calais via Coquelles, I should almost certainly have run into the enemy from the rear, with interesting possibilities. It was unfortunate that I knew nothing of Dick's whereabouts that morning.

I had some breakfast and now for the first time had a chance to look round our new position. The Calais-Sangatte road ran through the centre.

Stretching along the Company's left front was a ramp some 15 feet high, and from this position, it had an excellent field of fire over the flat country to the front. Only on the extreme left could the enemy advance unseen through a cemetery. The ramp had one big disadvantage in that it could be easily picked out as a target by the enemy gunners. The main road, which was blocked and guarded by French troops, led to a small village, half a mile in front, which might prove a useful forming-up point for the enemy.

On the right of our line some cliffs, rising sharply from the beach to about 100 feet, led on to a plateau, a salient of which ran out to the road opposite the ramp. The plateau was covered by shrubs and, both from the cover it offered to an advancing enemy and from the wide area it dominated, was a great danger and might be called 'the key to the position'. The French had concentrated their forces up there but they proved rather elusive. Our vehicles were parked in dead ground behind the salient.

Maurice posted the three motor platoons lining the ramp and my sections filled or stiffened up gaps where and when required. Company HQ was in an air raid shelter under the high ground – an ideal place. The high ground itself was left to the French but, to my knowledge, there was no close liaison with them and in retrospect it would seem questionable to have depended on them for the safeguarding of our most vulnerable flank. They were armed with the *mitrailleuse* – a heavier machine gun than our Bren. Some of the officers I met seemed good but I was far from impressed by the ordinary troops. They were obviously not from the best regiments and our opinion of their army as a whole was biased unfavourably by our having seen only their worst at their worst.

After breakfast I washed and shaved in a hut nearby. The noise of shelling to our front grew louder. Our gunners were bombarding enemy concentrations in the distance while the enemy directed all their artillery on ours which suffered heavily – and some enemy bombers silenced them for good later in the morning. The demoralised remnants retired through our lines without arms. They said that the enemy artillery and air bombardment had smashed their guns to bits and very few had got away alive. They described it as 'bloody murder'.

The enemy now turned their mortars on to our front; some shells were landing in our lines and some bursting high above our heads. The latter were ineffective and we soon came to disregard them while the others which landed in the soft sand were small and had little splintering effect. After a bit we could tell from the whine almost exactly if they would land in front of us or to the rear. Those which landed very close were more frightening as they were preceded by little or no warning sound.

Everyone was busy digging in. Maurice had started off early in spite of Sergeant-Major Child's horrified protest 'What, sir, before breakfast?' Soon there was a good line of weapon pits along the top of the ramp. My platoon was in reserve for the moment. I walked from one section to another, trying to look unconcerned at the shelling and thinking of the old saying 'no-one is ever as brave again as his first time in action'.

About 15.00 the enemy, who had assembled in a wood some 3 miles away, debouched en masse, advancing across some open country, before disappearing into dead ground. Through my glasses I could see them clearly and estimated their strength at about a battalion. They would have been an ideal target for artillery but now we had none and they were too far off for our Bren guns. The French opened up a rattling, but I think harmless, fire with their *mitrailleuses*.

Half an hour later the Germans reappeared closer, crossing some open ground in single file, about 30 yards between each man. They were just in range and everyone opened fire – the French fast and furiously. I told my platoon to hold fire as they were a poor target and our ammunition not unlimited.

Presently they reappeared closer still and now supported by machine-gun fire. Bullets whined in a continuous stream just over our heads or past our shoulders, as we lay flat on a mound. Despite the strong temptation to duck behind cover the Company, to a man, lay there steadily answering fire. Morale was very high and we might have been at Bisley.

I remember Corporal May, who was in his element, betting a packet of Players he would roll one over before me. I don't think either of us won the bet. A number of spare rifles and Bren guns seemed to have appeared from nowhere and all of us who only started with revolvers now had rifles.

In front of us was the company of QVRs whom I had seen in Sangatte earlier in the morning. They had withdrawn into Fort Nieulay, about a mile away. A wireless message came through from Battalion HQ that they were out of ammunition and water and would have to surrender unless supplies got through at once.

Maurice asked me what I thought about it. The idea thrilled me to the core and I begged him to let me go. Here was the chance I had dreamed of – a death or glory ride of the kind one read about at school. My whole life seemed a preparation for this great opportunity. I wasted no time in loading all the spare ammunition and water on to the carriers of Sergeant Coletta's section and gave out my orders. A guide was to meet us on the main road near some buildings which I knew and would lead us to the post which was somewhere between Sangatte and the Coquelles Road. We set off without delay.

Arriving at the rendezvous, I found no sign of a guide waiting –

only a few empty lorries beside the road. However I had my map, so turning off into a rough track we made for the fort. The track was narrow and sloped down on either side to a fairly deep ditch. To the right and left the country was quite flat, the corn very green and about a foot high. Coletta led the way driven by Thatcher, I followed 200 yards behind, with a third carrier in the rear. As he approached the fort I suddenly saw Coletta's carrier swerve to the left and come to a halt with one track in the ditch. I drew up alongside and saw that it was merely a case of bad driving. A carrier will always swerve towards the downward slope and Thatcher should have known better. Meanwhile, with one track 'going spare', he couldn't get out.

I told Coletta to get the third carrier to haul him out and went on alone as I had most of the ammunition and water on board. I stopped about 20 yards from the end of the lane wondering which way to turn to get into the fort. Nothing had been seen or heard to arouse our suspicions until Paine, my wireless operator, tapped me on the shoulder and pointed. I followed his finger and there, unmistakably, camouflaged by grass and bushes in the hedge to our front and pointing straight at us, was the barrel of a machine gun. I stared incredulously. Who lay behind – a rifleman or a German?

I hesitated for 30 seconds, when the question was answered. A German soldier stood up, ran across the path and disappeared. It happened so suddenly that I hardly had time to speak. I expected Paine to fire the Bren-gun automatically, but he didn't. So I pulled the trigger of my anti-tank rifle. Click: it was at 'safety'.

I told my driver, Bance, to turn round and we made off, back to the other two carriers. It was one of those 'snap decisions' that are based on impulse rather than reason, but considering the situation afterwards, I felt it would have been impossible for an enemy post to remain there, had the fort been still in our hands. In fact, as I learnt later, the QVRs had capitulated. As we drove back, small arms fire opened up on us from the fort. I found the third carrier trying in vain to tow Coletta's carrier out of the ditch. I asked him if he thought it would have to be abandoned, but he suggested my trying to tow from the other end. Working quickly and calmly under fire, he attached it to my carrier and out she came.

Then, one behind the other, I led us off as fast as possible. By now the enemy's mortars were trained on us. Two shells fell in the road just ahead and one just alongside Coletta's carrier. It was a gloriously exhilarating experience, driving hell for leather, shells bursting all around and knowing we were safe as houses except from a direct hit.

As we approached our lines, I stood up to show them who it was and, just as we arrived safe behind the mound, Thatcher's carrier broke down from over-boiling – it had been a great experience. We had failed to relieve the garrison and had missed an opportunity of killing at least one German but we had been terribly lucky. Had they realised who we were and got up their anti-tank weapons or mortars in time it might have been a very different story.

Later that afternoon, I was called to Company HQ for an important message. Maurice was away somewhere and Everard was speaking from one of my wirelesses on the left of our front. He sounded excited and a crazy conversation followed:

Everard: 'Hullo is that Tibe 1?'[Tibe was the Company call sign, Maurice's wireless being called Tibe 1, and mine Tibe 2 and 3]. Answer: 'Yes Tibe 1'. 'Is that commander Tibe 1?' 'No Tibe 2'. 'But I'm speaking from Tibe 2'. 'Yes but I'm commander Tibe 2'. Then in desperation, 'Look here, Everard, it's Phil speaking'.

Everard said that tanks had broken into 'B' Company on his left and unless he was reinforced, he could not hold out. I told him I would send a Scout Section at once but he closed down without acknowledging. I got hold of Dryborough-Smith and sent his section off as quickly as possible. Shortly after, Maurice arrived and I told him what I had done. Another message from Everard arrived as we were talking. There were some tanks under cover just in front of him. If we sent round some grenades he thought we might knock them out. I asked Maurice if I could take them round and he agreed.

Fairly bulging with grenades and full of hope I got on to the back of Perry's motor-bike and we raced up to the left flank. I ran up to Everard only to find that the tanks had retired. Dryborough-Smith's section was well in position; the situation appeared completely normal except for spasmodic small arms fire on the left and bullets ricocheting through the grave-yard.

While I was there we received a message to retire into the 'citadel' as soon as it was dark. I went off in a carrier to reconnoitre the route which was very simple. When I returned Everard told me to go to Jack Poole, commanding 'B' Company, to tell him we had received this message and say we were retiring at 1030 hours. This message could not be delivered by wireless as Jack's sets were all out of action. It would also have been very dangerous if the enemy had intercepted it.

Stupidly I set off alone on a motor-bike. A railway line had to be crossed; as there was no bridge I left the bike on the near side and set off on foot. Directed by some riflemen I got to Jack's headquarters where I found his second-in-command, Henry Scott. He told me Jack and the rest of the Company were already retiring into the citadel. He spoke in a vague and rather incoherent manner and was suffering from shell-shock. He said he too wanted Jack so we set off together.

One or two trucks and motor bikes were drawn up nearby and we tried one after the other. But whether they had been deliberately put out of action, or we were particularly incompetent, I don't know. They refused to start. We decided to go on foot and soon caught sight of some 'B' Company vehicles going round a corner. We shouted but they did not hear and, running hard, we reached the corner just in time to see them disappearing down another street. This continued for about a mile when we stopped in desperation with sweat streaming off our faces. I decided that, as Henry was going to see Jack anyway, he could perfectly well take my message which was out of date already.

I left Henry and it was the last time I saw him alive. I began to retrace my steps to pick up my motor-bike and hadn't gone far before I realised I was absolutely lost. I was always a by-word for losing my way but I seldom remember feeling more desperate. I took stock of where I thought I was, looked at my compass and set off with anything but confidence. It was now quite dark. Not far off the crackle of small arms and the crash of shells and falling masonry showed that things were still lively.

I must have been walking about a quarter of an hour when I came upon a broad road crossing mine. On the far side was the railway. But my difficulties were not yet over. A German tank or machine-gun post at the top of the street was pouring a stream of tracer shot down it. It seemed much worse when you could actually see the bullets. I waited for a pause and ran for all I was worth across the road, slid down on to the track and crawled under a truck. I was not hit and did not appear to have attracted attention and made my way cautiously along the far side of the trucks for about a quarter of a mile to where I had left the motor-bike. I expected to be spotted by a sniper at any moment.

Sure enough my bike was standing where I had left it. I made a dash for it, kicked the self-starter frantically hardly daring to hope it would start. To my surprise it roared into life and I shot off down the lane which led to my Company. I quite expected to find that they had already left for the citadel and, when I arrived where I had left Everard, I found the place deserted. I stopped to listen and thought I heard the noise of vehicles moving up on the Sangatte road. I was then surprised to meet the whole Company column driving from Calais back to the position they had just left. This was more than I could understand.

I later heard the true story. The Colonel had ordered 'A', 'B' and 'D' Companies to retire after dark to hold the inner perimeter of the town. Charlie Madden was told to ride through the Citadel to tell 'C' Company not to retire. He muddled the message and told 'C' Company to retire through the citadel and they did this. They were met by the Colonel, who abruptly told them to return to their old position. Luckily the enemy had no idea of the muddle that was going on a few hundred yards away and no harm was done. It had been a very busy day as far as I was concerned and I was thankful to climb into my carrier for the night.

Chapter 4

The Third Day – 25 May

I was woken up early next morning whereupon the whole Company set about digging and improving their positions. The Germans appeared to adopt a regular routine. All shelling stopped about midnight, when they presumably went to sleep and they would not start again until about 0700 hours after they had shaved and breakfasted. This gave us time to sort out the chaos of the previous night. Rifleman Barley came to me, hopping lame with a poisoned ankle. Luckily I still had a first-aid box which Mum had given me so I opened it up, squeezed out a mass of puss and dressed it. He said he never felt it again.

The shelling started punctually and was first concentrated on the Company HQ area and the vehicle park. One shell landed only five yards away from a carrier in which Swares was sitting. He was quite unharmed and I picked up the nose of the shell to put it in my carrier. It was an ideal 'paper weight'. Another fell two feet away from Tucker's motor cycle which, apart from a puncture, appeared quite undamaged. I think they were using 3-inch mortars which, except for direct hits, did little harm.

Of my three sections, Crowther's was between 10 and 12 Platoons watching the main road, Dryborough-Smith's in the gap where the railway ran out through the ramp, and Coletta's in reserve, keeping a look-out to the rear. We blocked the railway gap with some large ambulances which appeared to belong to no-one and I kept my platoon headquarters at this spot.

In a dip twenty yards behind me PSM Simpson had his 3-inch mortar – the only one in the Company. Simpson was a first-class soldier in peace time and had one of the best platoons in the Company. The 3-inch mortar had only recently been given to us and he had had little time to train the crew.

He was ordered to set fire to three huge oil tanks about four hundred yards ahead to deny their use to the enemy. One was already on fire, and great clouds of smoke rose belching forth. Simpson started ranging on his target and his shells were at once spotted by the enemy.

Without warning a deadly concentration of fire descended onto our area. Sergeant Corrie and two or three others, caught out of their trenches, were killed and several wounded. During a short pause, we started bundling the wounded into one of the ambulances. More shells fell and splinters whizzing amongst us wounded some more. Maurice arrived unexpectedly and started directing operations. Dryborough-Smith and Harcombe volunteered to drive two ambulances to the Regimental Aid Post in the town while Perry climbed into the back of a blood-soaked one to dress the wounds of those unable to help themselves.

It was a horrible sight and the first time that we came face to face with death. I examined the dead to make quite sure there were none left alive. They were terribly distorted and disfigured – Corrie, especially, with his brains blown out. Some of the riflemen were badly shaken. Sergeant Dolmus shouted across to me 'What do we do now, sir? We can't carry on at this rate.'

I shut him up quickly and told him that, unless ordered to retire, we stayed there to the last man. Simpson had also gone to pieces and it was clear that he would never get his mortar to fire within a hundred yards of those oil tanks. His crew had suffered heavy casualties. Once he stopped firing the enemy, thinking they had neutralised the position, turned their attention to other targets and everyone soon became more cheerful.

The refugee problem however was growing worse and worse. Many had flocked out of Calais and others had retired before the advancing Germans towards our position. Finding a company of British troops who all seemed calm and confident, they decided that here was the safest spot and, try as we might, we could not get rid of them. There were a number of air raid shelters under the cliffs into which they were shepherded. They were very hungry and thirsty, and several mothers with babies kept crying out for food. The Colour Sergeant gave them what he could spare and I eventually persuaded my Belgian friend to try to control them. He had a ghastly job. I went into one shelter, where the civilians were packed tight. The stench was terrible and the noise of hysterical women and crying babies was heart-rending.

About mid-day, a number of German planes flew over dropping leaflets. They were written in French and stated that, unless all troops surrendered and marched with their hands up out of Calais to Coquille within one hour, the town would be bombarded by heavy artillery. I believe that German delegates, under a flag of truce, drove in to see the Brigadier, who naturally refused to surrender. A few leaflets were picked up by the riflemen who passed them round as the latest joke.

For an hour all shelling ceased, and an uneasy lull was broken only by a British reconnaissance plane flying low over the German lines. All their anti-aircraft guns opened up and we could see clearly the puffs of smoke, as the shells burst all round. The plane swerved continually, and it seemed a miracle that it survived so long, but at last one shell took its wing clean off. It spiralled gracefully down, crashing behind some trees, while the pilot jumped out and hovered over the scene in his parachute. Somehow it all seemed unreal, like watching a film. This was the last British plane we saw that day, air superiority having finally passed to the Germans.

The bombardment of the town started punctually and surpassed anything hitherto experienced in its weight and intensity. The shells from the heavy artillery caused great explosions, throwing up piles of earth and rubble which flew high through the air and landed many yards away. Every man crouched low in his weapon-pit, while shell fragments for the most part whizzed harmlessly overhead. I kept bobbing up to see if the enemy were advancing under cover of the bombardment, but there was no sign of movement. My own hole seemed of very inadequate depth and, in order to keep below the ground level, I had to squat cross-legged keeping my head bent well down.

The bombardment seemed as if it would never stop, but in fact lasted about two hours. Most of the shells seemed to fall in the citadel some two hundred yards behind me, passing quite low over our position. Stones and gravel were constantly falling all around, and one splinter came whizzing into my weapon pit, landing between my legs a few inches from a most vital part of my body. I put it in my pocket as a souvenir of a very 'close shave'.

As I sat there, cramped and alone, I had time to think of my family at home and to wonder what they were all doing at that moment. I was thankful that they could not see me. Hitherto I had felt quite fatalistic about death. Either God meant to spare me or he did not, and my life was in his hands. With plenty to do, it had seemed a matter of little importance. But now, waiting helplessly for the next shell to blow me to bits, life in the heart of my family seemed very dear to me. For their sakes I prayed, like I had never prayed before, that by a miracle I should be spared and I mentally resolved to make a real effort in future to live better and thus repay my debt of gratitude.

At last, after what seemed an eternity, the artillery bombardment stopped. Heads bobbed up out of the weapon pits and the men shouted to each other cheerfully. Our Company had been lucky, most of the shells having fallen on to the citadel where it seemed impossible that there could be any survivors. Those falling short had landed in the soft ground to our rear where the splintering effect was much diminished. Quite a number, too, fell with a thud but did not explode.

We were given little respite; soon the mortars started up again concentrating along the whole line of the ramp. From their whine we knew almost exactly where they would fall. One landed only two feet in front of my own weapon-pit, blowing it in on top of me. I had not heard it coming and lay bruised and winded, struggling for breath. My ears sang and for a few moments I lay there thinking this was the end. But I could feel no actual pain, so struggled out and looked round with a dazed expression. One or two riflemen stared in astonishment having given me up for dead, but, apart from slight concussion and deafness, I had no ill effects.

And now, to add to our troubles, rifle bullets started thudding into the ramp from behind. Whether they came from snipers who had somehow worked around, or from the French and QVRs in the citadel, we could not tell but the effect of being fired at in the back was most unpleasant.

One rifleman was hit in a railway truck just behind me and, thinking it came from the QVRs, yelled out, 'Hold your fire', and 'for God's sake hold your fire'. Corporal McBride unhesitatingly ran across and carried him on his back about 250 yards over open ground to Company HQ, while mortar shells fell all around him. He impressed me more than any other rifleman that I saw, and, with his cheerful voice and manner, did great work in keeping up the men's spirits.

One shell landed on my own carrier, ten yards from my weapon pit setting it on fire. The ammunition started going off at once, bullets fizzing in all directions and it was quite half an hour before it burned itself out.

Directly in front the enemy appeared unwilling to venture across the open ground. Occasionally we spotted a machine-gun post or a few men crawling up a ditch on whom we opened up. They disappeared invariably, so that it was hard to see if we had killed them. Only once did we have a really good target. About 500 yards to our left a party of about twenty ran across an open patch and were fired on by every available Bren gun. They fell flat on their faces waving white handkerchiefs. Through my glasses I saw to my horror that they were civilians and shouted to stop the firing, whereupon the survivors got up and walked towards our lines, still waving white handkerchiefs. It was a most unlucky incident for which they had no-one but themselves to blame.

Throughout the day we had no chance to eat or drink except from our haversacks and water-bottles. It was terribly hot and my lips were parched. The one redeeming feature was the French wine which my platoon appeared to have collected from nowhere. It was wonderfully refreshing and, whichever section I visited, I was offered a different kind of wine or liquor. Despite the fact that they had apparently unlimited quantities I never saw a single rifleman who had drunk too much.

More trying than the heat was the smell of mortar explosive, which lingered in the air, permeating our nostrils and lungs, until we could smell nothing else. The ground was bone dry, and the sand got into our boots, and clogged our weapons. But even in the most anxious moments, I saw riflemen dismantling and cleaning their Bren guns as calmly as they would have done on a barrack table.

Late in the afternoon Maurice summoned platoon commanders to his headquarters in the air raid shelter. He looked tired and worried and said the Colonel had told him he must fight his own battle and that he was thinking of retiring. He asked for our opinions. I said that

I had nothing to fear from my front where the enemy were being held. By retiring we could forfeit a very good position commanding the open country. In view of our casualties earlier in the day, I recommended the 3 inch mortar being moved further away, in order to prevent our suffering from any more concentrations directed against it. Peter and Pat were also against retiring and Simpson appeared willing to adopt any plan. Maurice agreed to stand there and moved Simpson's mortar which we all three shunned like the plague.

I went round my platoon telling them what I knew of the situation. It had been clear from the start that any idea of offensive action against the enemy's lines of communication must be abandoned and that everything must be concentrated on holding the town. It seemed to me that there were two possibilities. Firstly that the big counter offensive by the French army would cut off the enemy armoured units in which case our duty was obviously to hold out until they were dealt with. Secondly, if the counter-offensive failed we would probably be evacuated. The enemy were evidently far stronger than we had anticipated. In the distance constant streams of lorries and motor bikes could be seen but no-one dreamt that three armoured divisions had been brought up to take the town. I told my section commanders that we would stay in the present position and said I thought the enemy could not possibly keep up the present rate of shelling without running short of ammunition. I left them all in very good heart.

At about 1700 hours an urgent message arrived summoning me to Company HQ. Maurice met me on the way and said that the enemy were advancing in large numbers on foot along the beach. I was to take a carrier section and, advancing in extended formation, drive them back. He emphasised that there was no time to waste. Hurriedly collecting Coletta's section, I repeated what I had been told and we started at once. I had the impression that the situation was desperate and nothing but this suicide charge could restore it. One behind the other my carriers roared up the track which led on to the high ground, but on top things at once went wrong. Bance, driving my carrier, went at a steep bank without first getting 'square on' to it and his track broke. I jumped out and ran to catch up the leading carrier, just in time to see it disappear over the cliff. When I came up, I found that Thatcher had seen the danger only just in time and, by jamming on his brakes, stopped at an almost vertical angle. The crew climbed out, leaving the carrier balanced precariously.

The enemy spotted us at once and a hail of mortar shells fell all around with deadly accuracy. Johnstone fell a few yards from me and started writhing and jumping like a chicken knocked on the head by a car. I realised that any thought of reaching the beach must be abandoned so, taking the Bren guns and some ammunition from the carriers, I sent Coletta's – the only surviving one – back, with Johnstone inside. I posted Porter and Thatcher with the Bren guns into sand-bagged weapon pits, which were well-sited to command the beach. A whole string of those weapon pits had been prepared by the French some time ago, presumably for the defence of their coast. But against whom?

The enemy could be clearly seen 500 yards ahead concentrated in some shrubs on the beach. I ordered Porter to fire but, perhaps through shell shock, he had entirely lost the use of his limbs and could only sit there jabbering. I ordered Thatcher to fire, but his Bren gun was clogged with sand. I needed help desperately. The enemy had got our range exactly and mortar shells rained down very close, with sickening explosions. Those weapon-pits were a God-send but we had to have more men. I decided to leave Thatcher to clear his gun and go back to Company HQ myself. Porter was considerably worse than useless, so I told him to follow me. We crossed that hundred yards of open ground quicker than I would have believed possible – once or twice diving into a shell hole to regain our breath.

Reaching Maurice, I explained the situation as best I could and said I must have another Bren gun and two or three more men, if we were to hold on. He said he could only spare Gridley, the wireless operator, from his Headquarters, so together we climbed the steep slope, ran across that dreaded open ground and slid into the weapon pit. Our target was still there and with two Bren guns we let them have it. It was impossible to judge how many we knocked out, but they retired from their exposed position. Mortar shells continued falling all round us and rifle bullets whizzed very low over our heads. Some appeared to be coming from behind, but whether from snipers or the French I could not tell. I raised my tin hat on the end of a rifle to see if it attracted a volley of fire, but nothing happened.

Things now seemed more under control, so I sent Thatcher off to

Maurice with a message to say we were holding out all right. He didn't come back, and I never heard what happened to him. It was clear that we could deal with any attempted advance along the open beach, but the shrub covered slope of the cliff was in dead ground and a whole Company could have advanced along this to within a few yards without my being aware of their presence. The only place from which this ground could be covered was a clump of bushes some way out on the shore. It was impossible to reach this spot without crossing the open beach in full view of the enemy, and the bushes would be a wonderful target for enemy mortars. I was just weighing the pros and cons of moving one Bren gun crew to this spot when, as if in answer to my thoughts, a German bomber flew over dropping a heavy load of bombs on to it. Every bush and plant was blown high into the air and, when the dust settled, nothing remained but the shell holes.

Soon after this I noticed a British destroyer cruising toward the shore and, when about a mile off, it opened fire on the enemy positions. It then turned sharp back, but repeated the performance several times and its fire seemed very accurate. It was a comforting sight and made me feel I was not quite alone. Enemy guns engaged it at once, their shells falling quite close and sending up fountains of spray. Some aircraft also appeared, carrying out both dive bombing and low level attacks. The destroyer finally made off without, as far as I could see, receiving a single direct hit.

Gridley and I seemed to be in that weapon pit for ages. Between us, we had a Bren gun, a rifle and a revolver. I remembered that I had never fired the latter in my life and decided to do a little practice. Selecting a big stone some 30 yards off I fired and to my surprise the sand flew up only a foot to the left of it, so I rested on my laurels.

Gridley was superb. Our situation was far from comfortable and we were apparently isolated, but he was quite unruffled. He kept up a ceaseless chatter, taking an almost paternal attitude toward me and I wish our conversation could have been recorded. Earlier in the day, he had sat quietly in the headquarter truck, his ear phones on, taking down messages without a glance at the shells dropping nearby. In a moment when he had left the truck, it had received a direct hit and was gutted. So, with his wireless gone, he was only too grateful for another important job.

The time passed slowly and we prayed for darkness when we could once more regain touch with the Company. Now and again a target appeared, we opened fire and it vanished. The enemy seemed in no hurry and preferred keeping their distance rather than risk an advance over the open. Their mortars kept up a spasmodic fire but our weapon pit gave us complete protection except from a direct hit.

Our ammunition was running low, so I crawled out on my stomach towards one of my carriers. Passing another weapon-pit I discovered a *mitrailleuse* complete with boxes of ammunition. These I dragged back fixing the gun to a mounting, which was already set up, just in time to deal with some Germans crossing a gap.

As it grew darker our spirits rose. Presently a couple of Frenchmen crawled in and joined us, followed by two more, probably the crew of the gun I had taken. They said their company was posted out in front, but I could not understand their silence during the evening. They produced a bottle of strong liquor which was handed round. We were very hungry and thirsty and it did us a lot of good.

I persuaded one of them to take me forward to the advanced French post where I met their senior officer. He seemed capable and helpful and told me he had about eighty men under his command. He said he was quite confident that he could hold the high ground. I had not the slightest doubt that every one of his men had spent the afternoon flat on the floor of his weapon pit. Why otherwise had the enemy been allowed to advance along the shore, without a shot being fired? I kept this to myself, but emphasised the need to keep a watch out all night – '*Il faut absoluement maintenir des patrouilles toute la nuit.*' '*Oui, oui, mon capitaine, naturellement.*'

It was now quite dark, so returning with Gridley to Company HQ I told Maurice the whole story. He agreed to leave the French to guard the high ground during the night, promising to send up reinforcements next morning before daybreak. I found my other two sections in very good heart. Each time I visited them, I was struck by the same feeling of secret happiness at our mutual confidence. Before Calais, we had had little time to get to know each other and there always seemed to be invisible barriers between us. It was hard to define but I had not felt completely at ease with them – and vice-versa. But for four days now we had been together, eating the same food, sleeping together, sharing the same risks and hardships and a different and better relationship had sprung up. Now we knew each other down to the last detail and trusted each other accordingly.

Land-mines had been brought up, some of which Sergeant-Major Childs had given to Dryborough-Smith to block the railway. I said I would inspect them in the morning. Sergeant Floater had been detailed to convoy an ambulance full of wounded in to the Regimental Aid Post [RAP]. Before leaving he said he had been told the road was blocked by an enemy post and asked what he was to do if this proved true. I disbelieved the story and vaguely told him to use his own discretion. I saw him on his return when he told me he had no trouble.

About midnight I received an order from Everard to collect the water and ammunition from the two carriers up by the cliff. I told him I thought I could rescue the carrier which was perched precariously over the edge, by towing it back, but he decided that the operation was too risky in the dark and would almost certainly bring down a barrage of fire on our heads.

I detailed three men to accompany me and set off once more up the slope on to the high ground. We went in single-file with me leading as I knew the way. Peering through the darkness, the revolver ready in my hand, I kept imagining I saw figures receding before me and every bush looked like a machine gun post. I went cautiously forward to the French position where I found everyone fast asleep on the floor with no sentry out. I woke up the French Officer with whom I had spoken before, told him what I was going to do and once more impressed upon him the need to keep a sharp look-out.

We found our way to the carriers without being fired at by a Frenchman or meeting a German patrol. There was so much ammunition and water that we had to make two journeys. It was delicate work unloading the first carrier as it looked as if the slightest touch would send it careering down the cliff-side onto the shore below. How Thatcher had stopped it seemed a miracle to me. As we were finishing the job there was a drone over our heads and a bomber flew past. It dropped its load onto the docks about a mile away almost exactly where our company had been on the first night. The noise of the explosion shattered the stillness of the night and a great shower of sparks flew up all around reminding me of a firework display.

Our job finished, I reported back to Company HQ where I found

Martin. Except for Ted Barker, who had brought up the rations and ammunition from time to time, Martin was the first person from Battalion HQ to visit the Company. We were thrilled to see each other and I eagerly begged him for news. He said we could expect more support tomorrow from the air and sea which cheered us up. There were also rumours of a Canadian force on their way from Boulogne to relieve us but he knew nothing about this. Next day we learnt that Boulogne had been evacuated.

There was little news from the other companies. Derek Trotter had been reported wounded very early in the battle and 'B 'Company under Jack were said to have had some hard fighting against tanks. Our own Company's casualties already amounted to sixty. Although the situation was critical the inner perimeter of the town had not been pierced and I went to sleep in my carrier that night very, very tired but with no grave misgivings.

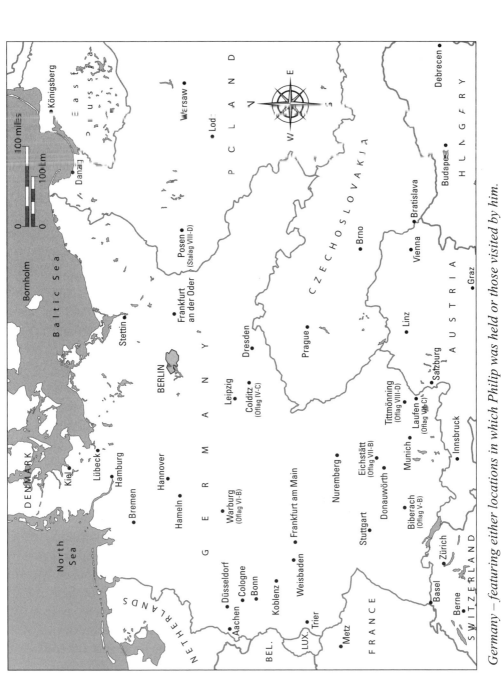

Germany – featuring either locations in which Philip was held or those visited by him.

Chapter 5

The Last Day – 26 May

It seemed as if I had hardly fallen asleep before I was woken up to see daylight already appearing. Maurice held a platoon commanders' conference at about 0700 hours. He told us to improve our weapon pits while we still had time and to hold our present position at all costs. Peter Parker's platoon was moved to occupy the high ground where I had spent such an uncomfortable time the evening before and Everard went with him.

I then went round my platoon. They were all in great heart and each section gave me something different to drink. Crowther alone seemed dispirited. He had never really recovered from the first night when, after moving out of the goods yard, dead tired, he was told to keep an all-night guard on the Sangatte Road. Through lack of sleep he seemed to have lost all initiative. I tried to cheer him up, giving him every reason why I was convinced the enemy would run out of supplies and we would be relieved.

The gap where the railway line passed through our position in which land-mines had been placed the night before still looked dangerous. The ambulances which had blocked the gap the previous day were gone so we decided to move a number of railway trucks into their place. For about three quarters of an hour we heaved and pushed on an empty stomach until the gap was satisfactorily blocked. The enemy made no attempt to hinder us although we were in their full view.

One of my couriers completed the job by towing a broken-down lorry into the last gap. Driving round in front of the ramp it returned behind our lines through a gap in Pat Sherrard's position which Perry had already reconnoitred on his motor bike. Tucker had disappeared during the previous day and I never saw him again. I heard later that he was wounded by a machine-gun bullet in the leg. Perry replaced him and was indispensable – never leaving my side for the whole day except to take messages.

The mortars started punctually at 0800 hours, shelling our position as hard as ever. Under their cover the infantry tried to advance but they were very cautious and seemed unwilling to take risks or come to grips. This exasperated Dryborough-Smith who loathed sitting down under the mortar fire. With fixed sword he raged up and down muttering 'Just let me get my hands on one of those bastards.' It seemed strange that they should try creeping forward now after an undisturbed night in which to improve their positions.

Here and there a Verey light was fired into the air such as we had seen on the first morning patrol. The forward troops were signalling to their gunners who usually replied by plastering our positions more heavily than ever with their mortars. The nauseating smell of explosives permeated the air. Despite the noise and discomfort, the sand in my clothing, cracked lips and scraped hands, I found time for a short sleep.

At about 1100 hours, above the noise of rifle fire and mortars, I heard a drone in the distance and, looking up into the sky, I saw about a hundred planes approaching in perfect formation. They looked just like a flight of wild-fowl flying imperturbably at a considerable height. I watched fascinated. They were almost overhead when, one by one, they detached themselves from the main body, diving vertically and, as it seemed, straight for our positions, omitting a terrifying wail. It looked as if they must crash into the ground but a few hundred feet up they released their bombs, which could be seen clearly, sometimes one or two at a time, sometimes even four. For a moment it looked as if they might overtake their bombs but, at the last moment, they flattened out roaring close over our heads, before climbing back up into the sky; meanwhile their bombs exploded with a deafening roar and threw up clouds of debris unlike anything I had ever seen before.

At first the effect was paralysing as the wail of their sirens – for they must have had sirens fitted somewhere – struck terror into our hearts. Each pilot seemed to make straight for one's own weapon-pit and each load of bombs seemed attracted towards one, as by a magnet; after a few moments, however, it became clear that the citadel, 200 yards in our rear, was their main target. Heads popped out of weapon-pits to right and left as the riflemen began to realise that their psychological effect was far worse than their sting. Here and there a Bren-gun was hoisted on to its mounting and soon there was a crackle of small arms fire as each rifleman tried to hit back. On our right one or two planes were diving over the sea but their targets were out of sight behind the cliffs.

Whether any were shot down I am not certain. Several times a plane diving straight toward the earth disappeared, and I waited for the crash but it straightened up in the nick of time and soared serenely back into the sky. Throughout the bombardment there was no sign of a British fighter. We prayed for their arrival constantly because they would have found those dive-bombers an easy prey. Although the noise must have been clearly audible in Dover no plane was sent to our aid and I realised months later that every available one was being used at Dunkirk, 20 miles further north, where the evacuation of the BEF had already begun.

At last after what seemed an endless H.G. Wells nightmare, the last bomb was dropped and the planes made off whence they had come. The bombardment had in fact lasted little more than half an hour, and, being concentrated chiefly on the dock-area, the citadel and the centre of the town, 'C' Company had come off comparatively lightly. We were not left long in peace. The mortars, which had been silent during the bombing, now started shelling our positions intensively. The heaviest fire fell on the high ground to the right. Here the enemy advanced in force; after the French position was overrun Peter Parker's platoon, including all available headquarter personnel, never stood a chance. A Frenchman ran forward with a white flag and was at once shot dead by Corporal Marks. Next moment both he and Corporal Booth had been blown to pieces. They were both great chaps, close friends in peace time, and they fought superbly throughout the battle. Everard and Peter were taken prisoner and the remainder quickly overwhelmed.

The enemy were now in command of all the high ground overlooking the Company position, which they could enfilade from the flank and rear. There was only one thing to do. Maurice ordered a general withdrawal of the whole Company back to the goods-yard area where we had spent part of the first night. There was no time for detailed orders to my section commanders. The enemy were firing steadily on to us from the high ground and the Company had already begun to retire on the right. I told everyone in my area to take their weapons and as much ammunition as they could carry and get back as quickly as they could.

I noticed Sergeant Delmus near me, looking completely calm and unruffled, so I told him to stay behind with me and cover the withdrawal. We each had a Bren gun with which we fired burst after burst from different positions as we hoped to deceive the enemy into thinking the ramp was still held. Then, having given the rest of the Company time to reach the goods-yard, we packed up and made off as fast as possible.

I was running about ten yards to the left of Delmus when I heard the whine of an approaching shell. We both fell flat on our faces, the shell landing exactly between us. There was a deafening explosion and I heard the fragments whizzing close over my head. I got up choking and could see nothing in the dense cloud of dust. I shouted to Delmus and to my relief he answered from quite close. He also was untouched. We ran back stopping now and then to fire a burst at the enemy. Luckily our line of retreat was hidden from those in front by the ramp but from the high ground on our flank every movement was overlooked.

Passing the citadel the French called out, 'Why are you retiring, why are you running away?' I shouted up to them 'It's all right, we shall come back. Don't worry.' Having arrived safely at the goods-yard I felt ready to drop. It had been a long run carrying the Bren gun and, like the preceding days, it was terribly hot. Parched with thirst, imagine my amazement when I saw a large barrel of red wine through which a shell splinter had smashed a hole near the top. After rolling it over I lay on my back while the wine poured out, lapping over my face and neck, and I drank to my heart's content. It was an ecstatic feeling and, much refreshed, I made my way through the yard into the street where most of the Company were waiting – either in shops or cellars.

There I met the Colonel, Alec Williams and Mike Sinclair begrimed and almost unrecognisable with four days growth of beard. They showed me a large building near the docks into which 'C' Company were to assemble while a small covering party stayed back to block the street. Maurice was nowhere to be seen but I soon found Pat who, during the retreat, had to swim across a canal. I told him to get the Company organised inside this building while I stayed behind to guard the street.

The noise and atmosphere in the town were indescribable. Mortar shells were falling all around. Every other house was on fire and clouds of smoke and dust made it hard to breathe. Had it not been for our anti-gas eye shields, we could not have kept our eyes open. Moreover from time to time great slabs of masonry, dislodged by fire or mortar shells, fell crashing into the streets crushing anyone underneath. Perkins, the Ordnance Officer attached to the Battalion, died in this way.

I got my rear-guard into their positions; Lance Corporal Johnson and Rifleman Welch were to guard one street, Sergeant Dryborough-Smith and Lance Corporal Brown another, while Rifleman Swares, Perry and I got into a large shell crater in the middle of the cross-roads. As soon as everyone was in position Maurice arrived and I told him what I had done. He said that 'A' Company was withdrawing into the same large building and that, as soon as they were all there, I would be relieved. I presumed that we would try to hold out until night-fall and then would be evacuated by sea.

I found one or two from 'D' Company in the streets to reinforce my party. Sergeant Roxman with his head bandaged was in very good form. We had been on the same drill cadre just after I joined the regiment and, being a racing enthusiast, he had plied me with tips of horses that just could not lose. Now, wounded and in the heat of battle, he asked me grinning 'Had any good winners lately, sir?'

One of my chief difficulties was caused by the refugees. Hundreds of women and children, and not a few French troops, were wandering meaninglessly while hysterically shouting and weeping. They prevented me seeing anything so I tried to usher them into cellars, shouting callously at them, but they paid little attention. Unavoidably many were shot.

Among the crowds I noticed two riflemen supporting another who had been wounded with uselessly dangling legs. I suddenly recognised Alan Wigan. He was the same as ever, not quite knowing what was going on, looking round dazedly and joking in his own querulous way. He was wearing no shoes and a rug was wrapped round his waist in place of trousers. The riflemen said he was badly wounded, with half a dozen machine gun bullets in the leg, but Alan would not hear of it. I wished him good luck and the party staggered on down the road.

Shortly afterwards I heard a shout from behind and saw Maurice waving in my direction. I took it that 'A' Company had withdrawn into the building and that I was to come back. I called in my riflemen and, arriving back, discovered Maurice having a scene with Colonel Holland, whom Colonel Miller had succeeded as 'Commander of Calais'. I gathered that Colonel Holland was telling Maurice he had got 'wind up' and that the enemy were nowhere near. His final words were 'I shall go off to see how they are getting on in the citadel. What's more, I shall take my mackintosh.' Exasperated by this doddering old man, Maurice turned round to see me, framed in the doorway. Apparently he had been waving to somebody else and had had no intention of recalling me. For several minutes he never drew breath, calling me every sort of bloody fool he could think of, and insinuating that it was I who had 'wind up'. This was too much for me and I had the utmost difficulty in controlling my temper.

The scene blew over and I returned with my rear-guard to our old position by the crossroads. I sent one of them to search the shops for something to drink, as we were again terribly thirsty, but little could be found as every restaurant and shop had been smashed and looted.

Swares lay beside me with his Bren gun, absolutely calm. Back in England I had found him very quiet and hard to get to know, but here his best qualities came out. Nothing worried him. Occasionally he made a remark with his slow sense of humour and I realised I would rather have him with me than almost anyone I knew. Our field of fire was restricted but from time to time we saw a few Germans creeping forward. Once a mortar detachment gave away its position by firing a Verey light and Swares opened fire. It was impossible to see the result but there was no more movement from there. Once Maurice went forward with Sergeant Cash, both armed with rifles. They returned a few minutes later saying they had killed four Germans.

Away to the right on the cliffs we could see some movement. Sections were running forward, stopping, and running again. It was difficult at first to identify them but soon we saw they were wearing the square tin-helmet of the Germans. Swares swung his gun round and sprayed the slope of the hill with fire. It was now clear that the enemy had broken through along the sand dunes from the north as well as the south. Colonel Miller arrived to say that, as we were surrounded from every side, further organised resistance was impossible. He ordered us to break up into small parties and try to escape as best we could.

For the moment I could not realise the importance of what he had said. I had become accustomed to the possibility of defeat but assumed that we should hold out until evacuated and, if that was impossible, defend to the last man and the last round. This phrase had been a by-word at Sandhurst, where the word surrender was unknown. Here in Calais, despite its dramatic nature, it seemed the simpler alternative. A soldier, who is given a task and told to hold out to the end, finds this easier, provided there is no panic, than casting himself loose from his battalion and fending for himself.

In a daze I collected my party into a cellar, repeated what the Colonel had said, and tried to consider our best plan. My mind was in turmoil and it was difficult to think coherently. Organised resistance was finished and the enemy tanks might roll up at any moment. For a while everything seemed useless and death inevitable. This thought was exacerbated by the scenes of horror we had lately witnessed and by the inferno raging all round. Then I recalled the words 'escape in small parties' and considered the best way. The Colonel had said he was going south but I remembered hearing a strong rumour that Boulogne had already fallen. I had heard nothing of Dunkirk but in that direction there seemed to be a small chance.

It would be impossible to make our way along the beach as we had already seen German troops advancing along the cliffs from the north. The only hope lay in making our way through the town. I took out my compass and fixed the direction in my mind. Then splitting the riflemen into two parties of six, I set off with the first group. We moved well dispersed on either side of the street. In front was a barricade of vehicles and furniture pulled high and burning furiously. The air was thick with smoke and dust from the falling masonry and the background was one of exploding shells and crackling small arms fire.

We turned off down a side street, then back on to a main road, checking the direction from my compass at each corner. We had gone about half a mile, when the road opened out in front into a large square. I peered cautiously round the corner to see several tanks. Some Germans had dismounted; two of them were studying a map while another was doing something to his tank.

They were only a hundred yards off and I watched them for a minute, until I was spotted, I saw them jump towards their tank but waited no longer, darting back with my section up another street. After we had gone a few yards, round the corner in front swung a German tank and I realised we were trapped.

In a flash we dived, one behind the other, into a cellar and ran up some stairs onto the first floor of the house where we lay panting on the floor. We could hear the approaching tanks which stopped just below. After a pause machine-gun fire sprayed the inside of the cellar with stream after stream of lead. The noise was deafening and the whole house shook. Another pause followed while, sweating with fear, we waited for the gun to turn upon the first floor of the house where we lay stretched along the ground. But the tanks moved on down the street and, to our unspeakable relief, we realised that, for the moment, we were saved.

We lay still for some time, thanking God for our escape and then I got up and moved quietly to the window looking cautiously out through the muslin blinds into the street. The continual stream of tanks and lorries passing below was being directed by a German at the cross-roads. A group of Germans stood by the corner studying a map and from time to time the one with the map gesticulated or pointed down a street. I thought what an easy target they were for us. With six rifles we could kill six of them with no difficulty by firing simultaneously out of this window.

I drew back into the room and tried to make up my mind what we should do. Provided we were left undisturbed the solution was easy. We would wait until it was dark and then steal out in pairs, and try to reach the north edge of the town. If we were lucky we would make our way up along the crest towards Dunkirk. But should we go armed or unarmed? Should we be prepared to fight our way out of the town?

What seemed much more likely was that there would be a house to house search. What should we do in this case? It would be easy to hide behind the door and knock anyone who came through on the head. If necessary I could use my revolver. But the victim would be missed and our presence soon discovered. Should we hold out in this house, firing through the doors and out of the window, to the end? These and many more problems flooded my mind. For the first time I felt the whole weight of the responsibility for the lives of three riflemen. It was unfair and cowardly to discuss the problem with them. I must decide it for myself.

Unwillingly and, as I felt, weakly I decided that I could not sacrifice their lives for the sake of prolonging resistance. We could certainly kill at least half a dozen – perhaps more – Germans. But now that they had the town I decided that this was insufficient reason for our annihilation. I explained my conclusion which was accepted resignedly but have no doubt that, had I taken the opposite decision, they would all have fought to the last.

There was nothing now to be done, except wait for darkness, so we made ourselves as comfortable as possible and slept while we could. I woke up some time later and, feeling hungry, explored the house for food. The place was in a mess and looked as if it had already been broken into and there was no sign of anything to eat. I looked out of the window and, to my dismay, saw a party of Germans leaving one house and going into the next. It looked as if they were carrying out a methodical search. From time to time a shot rang out or there was the explosion of a grenade.

Everyone in the room was now awake and we listened anxiously. The grenades seemed to be going off close and occasionally we heard the staccato shout of a German in the street. Presently the floorboards creaked below and we realised that our turn had come. A heavy German boot sounded on the stairs. In order to prevent him throwing a grenade into the room, I stepped out and called *'Kamerad'*. The uttermost depths of humiliation had been reached.

Chapter 6

The March

We trooped downstairs, hands above our heads and with equipment discarded, while being continuously shouted at by our nervous and excited captor. Several Germans came running to his call and we were lined up and searched. Then, with our hands still up, we were marched down the road for a quarter of a mile until we came to a square. In one corner there was a plot of grass where a number of British troops were digging a large grave. There were several bodies lying on the pavements and in the road. On all sides were signs of havoc – lorries burnt out, buildings damaged, and down the gutter poured a flood of water showing that the main supply had been hit.

We were ordered to join the digging party. It was hard work as we were not only tired and hungry but the nervous reaction to our humiliation surrender had shattered most of us. Everyone moved as in a dream and the immediate future was impossible to contemplate. It seemed as likely that we should be lined up and shot as that we should be marched off to Germany. It did not seem to matter which alternative was to be our fate. The zest for living and the fear of death had been replaced by a stupefied indifference.

Someone pointed out to the Germans that I was an officer and I was told I need not dig. The grave was almost big enough anyway – about six feet by ten, but quite shallow. We began to collect the corpses. It was a ghastly job. Many had been dead for two or three days with rigid bodies and their expressions fixed as in the moment of death. Some had been burnt in lorries and their remains could only be brought to the grave in shovels; the stench from these was unforgettable.

I searched the bodies for their identity discs. Very few wore them round their necks and delving into their pockets gave me a feeling of nausea. In one I found a golden purse, which in my muddled mind I preferred to bury rather than risk it being taken by the Germans. There was only one rifleman whom I recognised and he was from my Company. He was always in trouble in Dorset, but now his worries were over. *De mortuis...*

We shovelled the earth over their bodies. There was scarcely enough to cover them but we managed somehow and planted a rough cross, on which we scratched the name of those who could be identified, at the head of the grave. I felt I should conduct some short service or at least offer up a prayer for their souls but, with no book to guide me, to my shame I left it unsaid.

Nearby German soldiers were burying their dead. On each grave they planted a wooden cross on which they placed a steel helmet. The result was far more impressive than our poor effort.

To our surprise the Germans then produced some soap and spotlessly clean towels; we washed ourselves in the water which flooded down the gutter. Across the road some Germans were laughing and drinking in a bar. I asked if I could get some wine for my party who were all very thirsty – and this was allowed. I had spoken no German since leaving Eton and I could only just make myself understood. As we refreshed ourselves the German soldiers came up and talked to us and, even in my dazed condition, I was impressed by their smartness and manner. One pointed to my shoulder badge and said, 'KRR – King's Royal Rifles – *Sehr gute Regiment*'. Another started talking over the war and the destruction all round. '*Warum was es notwendig?*' he asked. '*Gegen England wollten wir nicht kämpfon, aber jetzt müssen wir auch Ihren Insel besetzen.*' 'Why was it necessary? We didn't want to fight against England, but now we shall have to occupy your island.'

That an NCO should know my regiment from those letters staggered me. I was also astonished at their efficiency and confidence. There was no hurry, no muddle, every man looked clean, shaved and healthy and knew exactly what to do. They seemed to bear no animosity against us and only showed surprise that we should have declared war on them; it was an accepted fact that England would be occupied within a few weeks. I pointed out a few errors in their argument, especially as to the latter, but was surprised at their complete confidence in and loyalty to Hitler. They were very different people to what I had been led by our newspapers to imagine.

It was getting dark when our party of about twenty was marched off to the church in the centre of the town where we spent the night. The church appeared to have suffered little damage from the shelling but inside we were met by a revolting spectacle. It was crowded with troops, mostly French, who were sprawled everywhere. With the abrupt cessation of their normal life these people had discarded their standards of behaviour and decency. The floor was littered with excreta and the troops seemed to care as little where they relieved themselves as to where they lay.

I saw no-one whom I could recognise and, believing that I alone of my regiment had surrendered without a fight, I felt more depressed than I had ever been in my life. I lay myself across two chairs and was soon mercifully relieved of my gloomy thoughts by a deep sleep.

Next morning, while exploring my temporary prison, I bumped into Mike Sinclair. It was wonderful to know I was not alone and he told me that Derek Trotter and Godfrey Cromwell were there too. Godfrey, wounded in the eye and side, had also been through another unpleasant experience. During the battle he had arrested the Mayor of the town who had tried to go over to the enemy and, as soon as he was freed, the latter set about getting his revenge while at the same time ingratiating himself with the Germans. Only after a stormy interview with the German commander did Godfrey clear himself.

At about 1100 hours we heard shouts of '*Aus, auf, los*' – words that were to haunt us during the following weeks as the signal for the start of the day's march. There were few preparations that we could make. I secured a French book that I saw lying about and managed to fill a bottle with water. Out in the streets we joined a long column and the trek to Germany began. My memories of the events of the next few weeks are very vague. I jotted down a few notes at the time and, several months later, I wrote an account of the journey which was subsequently lost. It was only four years later that I again sat down to the task of recording that grim experience.

We started off as a comparatively small column consisting mainly of French troops stretching for about a mile along the road. At intervals of about forty yards a German guard walked pushing his bicycle while German patrols bicycled up and down the line at irregular intervals. A lorry, on which a machine gun was mounted, brought up the rear and picked up those who were physically incapable of marching.

As we left the town, Godfrey who, though blind in one eye and going lame from his other wound, was remarkably cheerful and pointed out to us the position which his company had held during the battle. On the railway line a Red Cross train was drawn up riddled with machine gun bullets. In a cattle truck there were a number of dead horses. There were several carcasses of horses and cattle in the fields and the stench emitted by their inflated bodies was nauseating. All along the roads were derelict vehicles, some still smoking, while the ditches and fields on either side were littered with abandoned equipment and occasionally an unburied body.

The first day we had a light march of about twelve miles, stopping for the night at Guines where, four days earlier, the Battalion had intended to rendezvous. We were put into a church and during the evening for the first time we had an opportunity to consider the situation and discuss our prospects.

The most immediate problem was food. Most of us had been so pre-occupied in the last five days that we had eaten practically nothing. With our nerves keyed up to a very high pitch and our minds wrestling with so many pressing problems meals had seemed of trivial importance. But with the subsequent reaction, and the knowledge that we depended almost entirely on the Germans for food, our stomachs began to gnaw at our bodies. At Guines we were given a few caraway biscuits and Godfrey, who was an incurable optimist, insisted on sharing his own ration of chocolate with Derek, Mike and myself. I instinctively feared the worst and kept my chocolate for a last emergency and, although it was never needed as such, my fears proved terribly true.

We were all more worried about the fate of the rest of the Battalion than we cared to admit. We consoled ourselves with the hope that the majority had already been marched off but in my heart I was convinced that many of the best would have preferred death to surrender.

The thought of escape was pressing on our minds and we discussed the question repeatedly. But there comes a stage when physical fatigue affects one's reason and judgement and then one is inclined to adopt the easier alternative. We all know it was our duty and, with the prospect of years in a prison camp as the only alternative, none of us had the least doubt that we would make the attempt. At the moment, however, the Germans were taking us in a south-easterly direction and, as long as this continued, we were enjoying the double advantage of going towards the Somme, which we presumed the French would hold, while standing a very good chance of being released by the French counter-offensive which we still hoped would cut off the Germans. These two arguments, together with the hope that we should soon feel fitter with increased rations and a rest, persuaded us to delay the attempt to a more favourable opportunity.

The next day we had a longer march to Marquise where we again spent the night in a church. We were very crowded and the only available space in which to lay our bodies was up by the altar. With a deplorable lack of reverence, I stretched myself out on the altar itself, while the others lay on the steps below. We were soon fast asleep but that night I had an especially vivid nightmare.

Believing that we were still fighting I sprang up only to fall some four feet right on to Derek's solar plexus. Derek was terrified. Thinking he was being assaulted, he leapt to his feet, waking up everyone all round and it was several minutes before they could make out, in the inky darkness, the cause of the uproar. My nerves were in a shocking state and, during the next few weeks, whenever a rifle shot rang out or a door slammed I leapt into the air.

The third day, after a tiring march, we arrived in the afternoon at a place called Le Wast. There, in a large greyhound stadium, were packed thousands of other prisoners. It was beginning to rain quite hard and, as we forged our way through the crowd towards the Grand Stand, to our great joy we saw about a dozen brother officers. We fought our way through and, in our relief at seeing so many who we had feared dead, we rushed from one to the other eagerly asking after those who were missing.

Despite hitherto fearing we might be the only survivors the number of those known to have been killed now seemed terribly high. They included Puffin, Henry Scott, Claude Bower, Charles Stanton, Richard Warre, Dick Scott, Martin Willan and Perkins. Nothing was known of Norman or Grismond. Charlie Madden and Alan were known to be wounded, and Martin had already escaped from the march. From my own Company I was relieved to find Everard and Peter.

In a group quite near us were some Rifle Brigade officers, including Terence Prittie, Tony Rolt, and Charlie Forester. Charlie told me that David Sladen had been killed. The reunion was an agonizing ordeal with our feelings torn between two extremes – joy at meeting friends we had given up for lost and sorrow at the news they gave us. Everyone was hungry. In one corner of the stadium there were two cookers emitting a cloud of steam. Presently a move in the crowd showed that their contents were ready. Somehow they managed to issue out to the starving rabble a 'hot meal'. My share was a lump of horse flesh, the size of a matchbox, with a little gravy. It was my first experience of this delicacy and, though tough and stringy, its distinctive sweet flavour seemed a great luxury.

At about 1800 hours the gates of the stadium opened and gradually the crowd moved out into a column four times the length of our original one. It was still raining but, as we marched towards our next stopping place, I managed to pick up a French great-coat and tin hat lying by the roadside. Most of us had started with nothing. Only the Colonel and Alick Williams had had time to equip themselves; knowing that Calais was to be given up they had burnt all the Battalion documents in headquarters and collected a few belongings.

After a twelve-mile march, the long weary column arrived at a small village called Hucquelieres. There was no hope of sheltering the whole column so the troops were directed into a field, where they spent a miserable night in the long wet grass, while the officers were shut in a church. The local padre did everything possible for us and brought us contributions from the whole village. We were doubly lucky in securing a place near the door of the church and being 'adopted' by a most charming French liaison officer who made it his job to see that all the regiment had something to eat. A little hot broth and a slim pâte sandwich did much to raise our spirits and, in gratitude, I gave our French friend one of my shoulder badges. The troops out in the field must have had a very bad time.

That night I had more hallucinations. Hearing the rustling of the straw on which we were lying I thought the church was on fire. I woke up Wally Finlayson who had the same impression. Later that night I again imagined we were still fighting and jumped up saying,

'We're surrounded. We must keep them out.' The nerves of the others were so highly strung that they at once believed whatever anyone else imagined to be happening.

We left Hucquelieres next morning; the villagers lined the road with buckets of water or red wine, giving anything that they could spare. Their generosity was something I shall never forget and some day, when times are happier, I hope to revisit that padre and his village.

During the next two or three days we continued moving south-east averaging twenty miles a day. The weather was very hot which was a blessing at night, but increased our fatigue and thirst on the march. In almost every village women came out of their houses with buckets from which we filled our water bottles and occasionally we got a little to eat. For the most part, the people showed no preference whether they gave or sold their food to the French or to us. We witnessed many touching scenes as the French passed through the villages that were their homes. A French man would suddenly see his wife watching sadly as the column wound past. With a cry he would break from the crowd and fall sobbing into her arms until moved on by a German sentry. For them, passing through their own devastated country, the calamity was far more poignant and overwhelming than for us who knew that our homes were still safe.

Unluckily our relations with the French were aggravated by a number of factors. In the first place they were invariably given preferential treatment by the Germans who thus cleverly tried to split us from our allies. Whenever any food was issued the French were called up first and, at one place, the French were ushered into some comfortable rooms for the night while the British were left outdoors in a cobbled courtyard. The normal German soldier showed no preference for the French – rather the contrary which showed that this policy was dictated to them from above.

Another cause of friction was that, whereas the majority of British officers and men were taken prisoner with their total possessions limited to the clothes they were wearing, the French appeared to have been more far-sighted. They obstructed the column as they staggered under the weight of bundles or suitcases that most were carrying. When not blundered into us they were often begging the Germans for a lift. At each halt, however, they opened up their belongings and tortured us with the sight of whole loaves of bread, lumps of cheese and tinned foods. We had, however, only seen their worst troops in action; the unimpressive performance of these may have convinced our biased minds that they had never intended to fight and that, while our friends were being blown to pieces, they were packing their bags.

These arguments at the time seemed unanswerable and anti-French feeling ran high. But it was lessened by our meeting individuals who were wonderfully generous and without whose help many of us would have never completed the journey. Our hunger grew worse every day. Passing a vegetable garden, we would fall on our hands and knees trying to dig up a raw potato which, if successful, we devoured there and then. Once I saw a dog, which had been dead several days lying in the ditch with a swarm of flies feeding off its wounds. For a minute I stared at it, hesitating whether to take it for food, before deciding that it was more than I could stomach. In each village a crowd surrounded every doorway begging for food. I had about twenty pounds in my pocket when captured, part of which I changed into francs, and often managed to buy a biscuit or a little butter or cheese and perhaps some milk. Mike and I kept together almost all the time, sharing what we managed to get.

Soon after leaving Hucquelieres Alick Williams disappeared. I had talked to him about escaping and he was evidently determined to but was handicapped by his feet which were in a very bad state. Francis Williams and Wally Finlayson left shortly afterwards followed, during a particularly long and arduous search, by Jack Poole. Soon after we missed Jack a number of shots rang out from behind the column and, for several weeks, we were uncertain as to his fate. Jack had been a prisoner in the last war and, for him, the future held no illusions. It was clear that he was suffering terribly and he left without a word to any of us.

Escaping from the column would have been easy for the guards were at such wide intervals that, at almost any corner, one could have slipped through the hedge or into a wood without being seen. But still we were travelling south and still we postponed the moment hoping that to-morrow we should find some food or be still nearer the French lines.

We arrived at Doullens on about the sixth day out of Calais and were shut up in a former girl's school. We were allowed out into the grounds which were surrounded by a moat. Peter Duncanson had joined us the day before. With a few others he had been thrust into a room where we were lying and, to his amazement, found himself beside his brother Robin.

Peter, Robin and I now joined a party which was taken to a nearby farm to fill our bottles with water. Here I discovered an old man who was prepared to sell us some milk. We thankfully filled everything we had and I asked if he had any food. He said he had a cockerel which I bought alive and kicking. This was a tremendous acquisition. I tried to kill it by wringing its neck, but it stretched like elastic and Robin and I ended up tugging at opposite ends. The unfortunate bird was just about to expire, when a horrified Frenchman rushed up crying, '*Il faut couper la gorge, eh merde alors, il faut dusaing*'. Apparently it was a French superstition that poultry are inedible unless bled. Back in the school we started to pluck the fowl; it was a far bigger job than I had imagined. Tony Stallard, who had an extensive knowledge of anatomy, took charge of the drawing operations but the bird was hardly in the stew pot before the cry of '*Aus auf*' told us that we were once more on the move.

For the first time we enjoyed a short ride in a lorry to our next destination, where we had no chance to eat our prize. All the next day, during one of our longest, hottest and most tiring marches, Peter Duncanson carried it in a sack on his back until we reached Cambrai. Here we were ignominiously marched 'on show' round the town. One incident remains vividly in my mind. An old woman with a large box of sweets started throwing some into the column. She was immediately surrounded by a hungry swarm of men, all trying like sharks to snatch some food. The good lady was so badly crushed and frightened that she dropped the bag, burst into tears and was only with difficulty extricated from the midst of this sordid rabble.

Cambrai was the first camp with any semblance of an existing organization. Godfrey had gone on ahead in a lorry and secured bunks and some water for us. His eye had been getting worse and worse. While on the march, though outwardly cheerful, it was plain from his staggering gait that he was getting very weak. Frequently he would raise his hand up in front of him, trying to test his eye but I think it was almost entirely useless. At Cambrai the Germans at last took him off to see a doctor and we never saw him again on the march.

Several of our troops had arrived there some days before and I was particularly glad to meet Rifleman Johnstone, whom I had last seen being carried away unconscious from the cliff on the third afternoon at Calais. He had been concussed by shell shock but was now quite recovered.

That evening the last obsequies were performed over my cockerel. I gave it to a French cook who brought it back, exquisitely roasted, to our room; the French, however, were forbidden to communicate with us. He was pursued by an irate German and I only just managed to sit down on top of the steaming dish before the guard burst in. There was a hair-raising search for our prize but at last he left and we settled down to our meal. It was the most wonderful moment of the whole march and, although my share was only a drum-stick, I shall remember the taste of that chicken as long as I live.

Next day we were off once more and we continued our weary journey in a north-easterly direction towards the Belgian frontier. The country was flat and monotonous with straight roads passing between fields of waving corn. Every few miles we met compact little villages and occasionally a solitary chapel surrounded by the immaculately kept graves of those who fell in the last war.

The camps in which we spent the night varied much – except in their filth. The Germans, usually considered the cleanest and tidiest of races, made no attempt to cope with the sanitary conditions. No pits were dug and one had to pick one's way through a mass of filth to squat perhaps beside a flea-ridden vagrant. It is needless to enlarge on the smell which permeated every corner of the neighbourhood.

One night we spent in a coal cellar, lying on a steep slope of coal. When anyone moved an avalanche was started, which hardly made for a peaceful sleep. The washing facilities were extremely limited and I dread to think what we must have smelt like. Rations varied from a small packet of biscuits, or a lump of stale bread, to a bit of horseflesh. Even though we supplemented this with what we could pick up on the march, I would never have believed that the human body could exist, let alone march, on such minute subsistence.

The Germans varied considerably but, generally speaking, the further behind the lines we got, the worse was the type we met. The exceptions were helpful, and would try to get us water when we were desperate with thirst, but the majority behaved like no people I had ever met before – yelling in staccato monosyllables and showing no human feelings whatever. Our Colonel, with Mike as interpreter, would try to interview the commandant, but made little progress. There were a few unpleasant incidents. In one camp a soldier was shot collecting firewood and a Frenchman was shot for stealing potatoes. Another was wounded by a ricochet from a German who loosed off in excitement but shooting incidents were rare and I was chiefly struck by their inhumanity. As a typical instance, a dog, running across a field, was fired at by several sentries amidst howls of laughter.

At various times a rough search for weapons, maps, etc. was carried out but with little method and it would have been simple to have retained any small object. I unfortunately lent my gold compass to a friend who handed it over to the Germans when told that a Frenchman had been shot the previous day for concealing a revolver. On the whole there were very few cases of petty thieving or pilfering of watches, rings, etc.

Every day took us further from the French lines and reluctantly we came to realise that we had missed our chance to escape. The best opportunity would have been at Doullens, where we could actually hear the guns in the direction of Abbeville but now it seemed that there was no hope of regaining our freedom.

In retrospect it seems inconceivable that we should not have taken the plunge while the opportunity still existed but the truth was that, far from getting fitter, we became progressively more tired and hungry until the mental effort to think beyond our stomachs became too great. We had no maps, very little idea of where we were and, as a final discouragement, placards were stuck up saying that anyone attempting to leave the column or found in civilian clothes would be treated as a spy. Mike felt much the same as I did, and as no senior officers were prepared to give us any advice, we staggered on in a mental coma, further and further away from the direction in which lay our only hope. Once across the Belgian frontier, a marked change in the land-scape could be observed. The flat open fields gave place to a more enclosed and undulating country and the houses in the villages were more widely dispersed. For two or three days we marched through the thick pine forests of the Ardennes. I particularly remember one afternoon ascending a steady slope for hour after hour and expecting, at every corner, to reach the summit but always being deceived by the false crests. The villagers in Belgium showed the same sympathy and generosity as those we had met in France. On our arrival in a camp they would bring all that they could spare and there were many mouths to feed.

The Colonel appeared the least exhausted of the officers in the regiment. He was always near the head of the column and by his energy showed us a great example. Derek Trotter found it very heavy going. His wound in the cheek had caused his forehead to swell right out and, with an enormous moustache, he looked like some angry towering buffalo. Many were suffering from blisters, especially Ronnie Littledale who had been captured almost naked after swimming across a creek and so was wearing borrowed boots and clothes. Robin Duncanson, and to a lesser extent Mike Sinclair were plagued with rheumatism; I was quite fit except for a pain over my heart which restricted my breathing and so could only sleep at night when sitting bolt upright. Everard Radcliffe, who had always treated route marches and other efforts to get fit with contempt, survived the march better than almost anyone else but suffered from constipation so badly that he could hardly eat and was much distressed by our envy of his condition. To us anything seemed preferable to this aching gnawing hunger.

One day we were given a lift for several miles in German lorries and trailers. It was a wonderful rest for our feet, and we hustled round corners at a terrifying speed, the trailers swinging violently from one side of the road to another. We passed a field in which lay the wrecks of a dozen German planes – bombed presumably before they had time to take off. On we hustled, over a rickety pontoon bridge through the lovely village of Dinant. Here a hill rises sheer like a cliff, decorated with rock plants and on the top was a castle. Silhouetted from one of the turrets was a German sentry in his steel hat, his profile clear cut, gazing far out over Belgium – a symbol of Germany's domination of the country.

The march lasted about a fortnight but it seemed like a lifetime and I sometimes wondered whether they would keep us marching until the last man had fallen down exhausted. After covering some 180 miles on our weary feet we arrived at Bastogne station where, after a hot thirsty day in the sun, it seemed a luxury to be crowded with over sixty others into a cattle truck. Many were suffering from diarrhoea and there was no room for even one man to sit. The train jolted uncomfortably all night through Luxemburg across the German frontier into Trier.

Looking back on those two weeks much of the bitterness and pain has passed with the passage of time and I am left with a feeling of shame. Like cattle we were driven and goaded along the road – exciting, by our total loss of self-respect, sometimes compassion and sometimes scorn from onlookers. Like cattle, also, our thoughts centred on our stomachs as we snatched a mouthful of food from the roadside; in our tacit acknowledgement of the rule of our temporary masters most of us made as little effort to leave the herd and strike out on a line of our own as would a flock of sheep. Hunger, fatigue and humiliation were our spiritual companions and it would be many months before the sores healed and our minds attained anything approaching the peace they had been accustomed to enjoy.

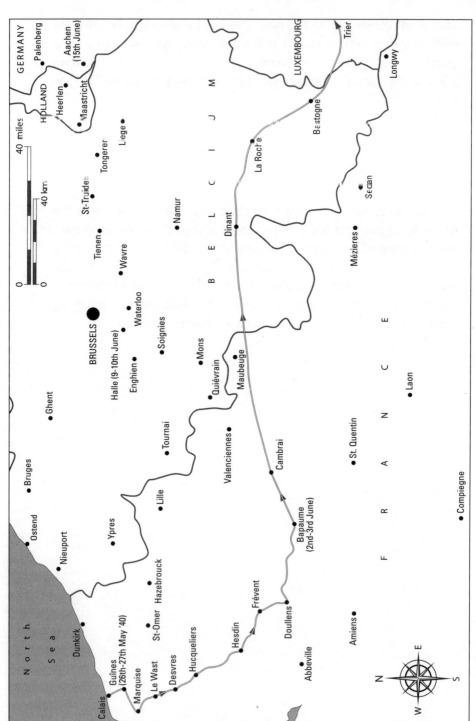

Philip Pardoe's march as a prisoner from Calais.

Chapter 7

Early Days of Captivity

In the early hours of this morning we passed through the broad clean avenued streets of Trier and, just outside the town, began a steep spiral climb to the camp which overlooked the town. There were many thousands of French and English troops crowded into the insect-ridden huts and the officers, after being searched, were taken into a big clean building where we spent several days. Now that the effort to march was no longer required a physical reaction set in and we spent most of our time on our beds. Hitherto we had only found one chance to write a note to our families – at Doullens, where the Germans gave little hope of the cards they gave us reaching England. Here we were allowed, within limits, to write as much as we liked. There was little we could say of the fighting and, apart from a list of those known to be killed or wounded, our letters were taken up with long catalogues of clothes, books and above all food which we urgently required.

Once a day we marched into the main camp for the midday bowl of soup. We were famished with hunger and the long queues waiting outside the cookhouse showed only too clearly that the troops were in a similar plight. Sometimes there were growls of dissatisfaction as those who had waited for hours saw the privileged column of officers marching up to be served straight away.

On these occasions we had a chance to contact some of the riflemen who were there. We had met many in the camps end route so that the Colonel was able to get some idea of our total casualties which we thought were about fifty per cent. It was as good as a tonic meeting them again and they showed a wonderful cheerfulness and not a little curiosity at seeing us, who had hitherto led such pampered lives, now weathering the same crushing experience in much the same crushing spirit as themselves. Sergeant Dalton, who was rarely without his bowler hat in peacetime, showed the same attention to us as when he was mess sergeant, but alas he had nothing to offer us now.

A week after our arrival we were once more on our travels, leaving Trier by train for Mainz. From the last camp we had a wonderful view of the undulating country, covered by such pine forests as I had never seen before, and now as we travelled in comparative comfort down the valleys of the Mosel and the Rhine, we passed those sloping hills on which grew the Hoch and Mosel grapes we had enjoyed at home.

The camp at Mainz was in the middle of the town. Shortly before our arrival, a French general had committed suicide in his room, hanging himself with a rope on hearing of the fall of Paris. The news of the armistice came as a crushing blow but, in a way, we were prepared for it by our own experience and by the unvarying stories of disaster from all the French with whom we talked, no less than by the German attitude which accepted it as a foregone conclusion from the start.

Our depression was lightened by meeting an airman, very recently shot down, who had been in England at the time of Churchill's speech on 4 June. From him we learnt of the evacuation of almost the entire BEF and, to our surprise, that the defence of Calais, far from the chaotic disaster it had seemed, was hailed in England as one of the epic rearguard actions of history. By drawing off three German armoured divisions it had allowed time for the flooding of the Dunkirk area and so had made possible the evacuation. Our joy at hearing that, far from being disgraced, we were the heroes of the hour did much to help us forget the needs of the moment and the grim prospect of the future.

We spent four days at Mainz, leaving our beds only for a midday blow-out of potato soup and a struggle in the canteen where, as at Trier, we could buy a little beer and a few articles such as cutlery and lavatory paper. The news that we were off to Laufen in Bavaria was welcomed by everybody for what little was known of that part of Germany had pleasant associations of snow-capped mountains and picturesque country-folk. Our journey in a cattle truck was uneventful. We had room to move about but could see little of the country; I remember it chiefly for my first lesson at bridge with some cards we had made out of biscuit cartons.

Whatever illusions we had concerning our stay at Laufen were abruptly shattered on arrival. Into a large barracks that had once been a castle were crowded over one thousand two hundred officers. The rooms in which we lived fed and slept, although varying in size, were packed with three tier beds. Apart from two enclosed courtyards, the exercise ground was limited to two fields known as 'the park', perhaps large enough together to hold three tennis courts. The canteen offered wine, beer, a few toilet articles and occasionally some fruit, but the whole of our pay, which for several months was halved owing to exchange disagreements, was barely sufficient to pay for the consignments of fruit, biscuits, and ice creams, which were available from time to time. The only redeeming feature of this camp was the view. The river Salzach flowed past the lower field and away up the valley could be seen the snow-capped Alps near Salzburg. Their appearance was never the same, changing with the atmospherics from day to day and even hour to hour and, by gazing at them, one could attain a feeling of peace and the realization that nature remains beautiful and aloof from the strife and cruelty of its inhabitants.

The actual conditions at Laufen were very depressing and it was hard to rid oneself of the feeling of being encaged behind the wire. From the very start we were oppressed by a 'convict complex'. Our heads were shaved close to the scalp like criminals and we were constantly reminded of our impotence in the hands of the enemy. As an instance, whatever the weather, we were habitually kept waiting up to half an hour on the morning parades waiting for the Germans to condescend to count us. This in itself would have merely fostered a hatred of them had not our senior officers adopted a passive attitude to such treatment. By using such phrases as 'our hosts' and by their desire to 'obtain more privileges' and their reluctance to fight for our rights, they caused a deep feeling of dissatisfaction among all ranks, which was not improved by the degraded and even dishonest behaviour of some senior officers who, deprived of responsibility, could think very little beyond their own selfish ends.

Our knowledge of the progress of the war was strictly limited to the German newspapers and their news broadcasts, so that, at the height of the battle of Britain, we knew that London was burning furiously but turned a blind eye to the possibility of invasion. There were roughly two schools of thought concerning the future. One, which was subscribed to by the majority, believed that a continuation of the war was as impossible as the defeat of Britain and that the only solution was a compromise peace. This idea was expounded with force by the Brigadier and Godfrey and particularly appealed to those who hoped to be 'home for Christmas'. The other school of thought, led by Padre Heard, argued that nothing but a peace dictated by Great Britain would be acceptable and that it would be in our country's interest if the war was still going on in three years time. The Padre was soon the most unpopular speaker in the camp but his arguments appealed very strongly to my instincts and reason. Amidst so much bad news, made more disquieting by the daily rumours of extravagant wishful thinkers, the Libyan offensive under General Wavell came as a breath of fresh air and, though our knowledge of its progress was limited to such phrases as '*Bengazi planmässig geräumt*', it had a most healthy effect on morale.

The depression caused by our environment was intensified by the hunger, both physical and mental, from which everyone suffered. The German rations for each day were about as much as we were used to eat in one meal and, until our stomachs shrank and parcels began to arrive, we were literally starving. Everyone looked emaciated, with sunken cheeks, thin limbs and potato-distended bellies. Climbing upstairs to the third storey of the building was an ordeal which had to be taken slowly, helping oneself up with the bannisters and, whether getting up from bed or from the ground after sun bathing, one had to pause a while in order to recover from the 'black out' which invariably followed.

Those who worked in the cook house and canteen were exposed to temptations they were unable to resist and the exposure of scandals caused much discontent. Tobacco was equally scarce and the incessant bartering gave greater scope to the unscrupulous while making it impossible for the rest to forget their needs. But one's faith in human nature was restored by the amazing generosity of many individuals. Jack Poole, for instance, gave a square of chocolate or some cigarettes to everyone in the regiment from his Hungarian parcel – one of the first to arrive in the Camp. David Fellowes and Nigel Payne, my old Blandford battery commander, asked me to help eat their first parcels and these are incidents I shall never forget.

Our mental hunger was in some ways just as acute. Up to the recent weeks our minds had been working at their top speed and now, finding themselves as it were in a vacuum, they sought any distraction on which to fasten. The restrictions on writing letters and the long wait and many disappointments until the unforgettable joy of the first letter from home, all this made us more desperate to find any subject of interest on which to concentrate. Books were few and those we could get our hands on were eagerly devoured. Church services were crowded as never before or since – everyone, whether habitual church goers or agnostics, flocking to give expression to their thankfulness for their own preservation and prayers for strength in the present and future. Lectures were given on every subject that can be thought of and every spare space in the camp was occupied by little groups squatting round their teacher, learning some obscure language, or by vast crowds listening and taking notes on agriculture or some other popular subject. Two lecturers I feel particularly grateful to – Joe Hume and Lynn Allen. By their talks on wine and shooting respectively, they succeeded more than any others in taking us out of our environment into a world of wonderful memories and associations. Concerts and sing-songs were frequent and in music, most of all, I found a peace of mind which it alone can give.

Up to now I have tried to paint a picture of the darker side of those days, but there was of course a brighter side too. After three or four months letters began to arrive from our families and ours reached them, establishing a contact with civilisation which did even more toward restoring our normal state of mind than the alleviation of our hunger. But this too happened gradually as almost every country in Europe answered the appeals which we were, for some time, too proud to send out. The British Legion in Switzerland did wonderful work sending exactly the food that was most badly wanted to vast numbers of prisoners. The British Red Cross took a long time to realise the magnitude of its task and not until it had been drastically reorganised did parcels begin to arrive in adequate numbers – luckily just in time for Christmas. Helped by the extra money sent from home we could at last afford some wine and, although there were most sordid scenes of drunkenness, intoxication brought a temporary oblivion which was well worth the after effects.

The regiment, on the whole, kept pretty close together; we had periodic dinners to which each brought his own food. Maurice, who had arrived at Laufen ahead of us, was more depressed than anyone I have ever seen. It was good to meet Grismond whom I had given up for dead. The sad news that Norman had been drowned trying to escape was confirmed but Betty was only officially told in February as, at the time, she was having a baby. I felt his loss more than that of anyone else since John died. Martin arrived several weeks after us and it was good to know he was alive. He looked terribly ill after his experiences in France. He did not stay long with us before being sent off to a nearby camp at Tittmönning in one of several parties of officers who, in the German view, were undesirable. All the others who had escaped from the march were already at Laufen when we arrived except for Alick Williams; months later we heard that he had reached England early in June and so was able to relieve our families of anxiety as to whether we had survived the battle.

I found myself messing with nine other Greenjackets most of whom I had known before and, except for much jealousy when the Rifle Brigade members got parcels earlier than us, we got on pretty well. Mike, Peter Parker, Peter Fraser, Peter Duncanson and I shared everything we received and for many months conversation veered round menus and restaurants. The urge to escape was suppressed for some time as all activity was forbidden until the first tunnel was completed. But only eight officers were allowed out, although some thirty could well have followed them, and the eight were all quickly recaptured. Ronnie and Mike started another tunnel but, through lack of self-confidence and initiative, I remained inactive. The desire to try and thus wipe out the shame of the march through France burned more and more fiercely but, although Everard and I made some feeble plans, the scope was so limited that without the necessary drive we would never have had a hope.

In the early spring of 1941 I caught chicken pox and, in the hospital half a mile away, I spent the happiest weeks of my prison life up to that time. On my return I was met by rumours of a move and, early in March, I was delighted to hear that I was included amongst some two hundred officers, mostly subalterns, who were off to Posen in Poland. I was sorry to leave many friends behind, especially Everard of whom I was very fond, but here at last was an opening – a chance to escape from this atmosphere of complacency and repression. Whatever our new camp was like it seemed to provide an opportunity to strike out on a new line.

After many postponements, the day for our departure arrived. I had discussed the prospects of the move with Peter Douglas, whose outlook on life was very similar to mine, and we decided to take any chance of escape on the journey. Philip Taylor joined our party and we collected food, maps and a saw in the hope of cutting through the railway floor boards. Despite the Germans' attempts to segregate us we managed, as the march to the station developed into a disorderly straggle, to get together into a 3rd Class carriage together with Chan Blair and Tony Rolt.

We set to work at once on the floor but, after several hours, decided it was impracticable. Tony and Chan were keen to escape to Switzerland while we favoured Poland, so we agreed that they should take the first opportunity to jump on the first day and we would try on the next. All that night they waited for a chance, encouraged by us, and all next day and night we kept ready encouraged by them; it was noticeable that the enthusiasm was always on the side of the party not trying to escape. In fact there was no chance for either party and, after forty-eight hours, the train drew in to Posen.

Laufen lay behind us forever with the memories of its over-crowding, hunger, depression and humiliation. But, as ever in life, the blacker memories soon faded and happier ones remained. These included the first letter from home, the first parcels of food and clothes, skating on the small rink we had flooded within snow banks in 'the park', and parties when wine and beer flowed; on New Year's Eve the commandant, who had arrived at midnight to stop the noise, was instantly surrounded by a ring of officers singing 'Rule Britannia' as a result of which Jack Fawous was arrested. The beauty of the snow-capped mountains and of the hoar frost made even the barbed wire attractive. Finally my friendship with Everard taught me above all the meaning of art and its relation to life.

Now we were in a different country and, as we staggered through the town sweating under the load of all our belongings, we looked eagerly towards the future. Once more our hopes collapsed as we halted within the high walls across a moat bridge at the dark entrance to an underground fort. The commandant, a swashbuckling Prussian, told us that we were to be incarcerated here as a reprisal for the treatment of German officers in Fort Henry, Canada, which this fort was said to resemble. As we trooped down the ill-lit, damp corridors into our rooms we realised that Laufen, compared with this, was a gin palace.

The next few days seemed black indeed. So overcrowded that many of us had to share a bed, bitten by fleas and lice until many people had septic legs, unable to read except on the window sill, mosquitoes rising from the overflowing sewers. This accumulation of horrors seemed at times unbearable yet the presence of General Fortune and Colonel Tod has a wonderful effect on all. They persuaded even the worst grumblers to see the brighter side of life and, by their attitude towards both the Germans and ourselves, they improved conditions, raised our self-respect and created a happier atmosphere; no-one would have thought of returning to Laufen, even had he been given the chance.

After a few weeks we were allowed up on to the roof – a welcome change from the muddy moat. The camp was thinned out by a party leaving for Thorn, parcels arrived to relieve our hunger and a small party was allowed out to work in a garden. With the improvement in conditions, our spirits rose, snow gave way to a warm spring and life seemed good after all. I bought a violin and continued the lessons I had already begun at Laufen and became really fond of it. With no wire round the camp the feeling of imprisonment became less oppressive but the coming of spring made the urge to escape ever more insistent. Peter, Philip and I joined forces with Ronnie Littledale [who was to escape from Colditz before being killed near Calais in 1944], Mike and Grismond in trying to tunnel under the moat but, after weeks of work on the trap we found that as soon as the earth was removed water flowed in, as it would on a beach – so we gave it up.

Then we discovered a room on the far side of the moat from which we planned to dig our way, but here again we were unlucky. Another party 'pirated' our plans, were most unfairly allowed to proceed and got caught. Ronnie, Mike and Gris at last found a way out early in June and let us in on their scheme. Only Peter Douglas, however, was allowed to go because he could fit into the wheelbarrow of a garden working party – and within a few days he had made it to England via Lubeck.

Then came rumours of a move and, once more, it looked as if we must try our luck on the journey. At the last moment Philip and I were offered a chance of a comparatively foolproof escape from the gardening party which, to our exasperation, the General refused to sanction as he considered it a breach of the trust which the commandant had placed in him. Thwarted whichever way we turned we armed ourselves for the journey with saws, pickaxes, maps and money; all these were hidden, evaded a search, and off we set once more. At the station we saw several long trains packed with war material which, coupled with rumours of troop movements and caricatures of Stalin, convinced us that war between Russia and Germany was imminent. On the platform we manoeuvred ourselves into a carriage as far as possible from the van in which the guards were concentrated and, after the usual delay, the train pulled out of the station.

We started work on the floor at once but without undue optimism for, although better equipped than the previous time, we knew the difficulties. To our surprise we found that our carriage, which was made in Holland, was different and within a few hours a large hole had been cut in the double flooring and, below us, we could see the railway track flashing past. We sat down to decide on the best plan of campaign.

We knew that our destination was Biberach, in the Black Forest and we calculated that the journey would probably take forty-eight hours. That meant two nights in the train – one near Berlin and one probably in the Danube area. At each halt we observed the drill carefully. The German guards poured out of their carriage to line both sides of the train. When we were about to move off the *Feldwebel* would shout *'Einsteigen'* and there would be a rush back to the guard's van. In this interval it should be easy to slip through the carriage floor on to the line and let the train pass over our bodies. By night it looked like a racing certainty. If we found that the train made faster progress than expected we still stood a good chance of escape in daylight provided the train stopped outside a station. We selected a place 150 miles from the Swiss frontier called Donauwörth and would take the first available opportunity after reaching it.

We slept in moderate comfort that night, while Tony Rolt and three others made similar preparations in an adjoining compartment. They agreed that we should be the first out using their exit as well as our own, and that they would follow at the next opportunity. We also agreed that four was the best number so Jack Hailes joined Mike Scott, Philip and myself.

Next morning we busied ourselves with final preparations, blacking our clothes with boot polish and sorting out our food and other equipment. The train put on steam and by lunch time it became clear that we would arrive before nightfall. This was a disappointment but not too discouraging At about 1600 hours we had just started eating our tea when the train clanked to a standstill. Tony put his head out of the window and said 'We're just outside Donauwörth.' 'God! Already? What's it look like?' 'Hell of a big place.' Then suddenly, 'My God, this is an absolutely ideal spot to do it. Right out in the open, no houses for half a mile – what about it?'

I looked out of the window with a queer sinking feeling, half of my mind seeking excuses to put it off, the other voice urging me on. The conditions looked ideal. 'My God, yes,' I said, trying to sound more enthusiastic than I felt, 'We'll have a crack at it.'

We crammed a last sandwich into our mouths and waited. '*Einsteigen!*' we slipped noiselessly through the floor on to the track, our bodies pressed close to the ground. I was nearest to the engine and lay facing it. Jack was next to me, and like the other two decided to face the tail. Hardly daring to breathe, but deafened by the thumping of our hearts, we lay waiting for the train to move.

Suddenly Tony's voice from above our heads – 'Look here, it's absolutely O.K., nobody's seen you or anything, but the guards have got out again. Lie quite still and they won't see you. It's absolutely all right.' Then Francis Williams' voice, 'Phil, Phil, send me some parcels from Switzerland.' 'Blast your bloody parcels,' I thought, then 'Oh, Francis, if I get away, drop Flick a line will you? Tell her there's nothing to worry about, if she doesn't hear from me for a bit.'

We lay still and waited. We were feeling calmer and more confident now. Tony kept up a running commentary: 'It's absolutely all right, boys. They haven't seen you. Just lie still. The nearest guard's about thirty yards away. I'm sure you'll make it all right. Never been more confident in my life. Everything's fine.'

Then at last, '*Einsteigen.*' My heart leapt with relief. I glanced round at the others but could only see Jack's boots. They were very still. With a lurch the train started moving. Next minute there was a loud 'plopp' close to my left ear. Someone, meticulously obeying the regulations, had waited for the train to move before pulling the plug. It had missed my head by inches.

I shifted a bit and glanced up at the train moving noisily and jerkily over my head. So this was what it felt like to be run over by a train. I had often wondered about it as a child and had felt a fascination for the experience – to lie down on the line while an express roared overhead. But this was absolutely easy. There was ample clearance over my body and the train seemed to be crawling. Even if one of those coupling hooks, which had looked so menacing dangling down, had reached my body, it would have been simple to move out of the way or push it aside with my hand.

The train seemed to be of immense length and, as the last carriage drew away, I glanced quickly up to see if there was a Bren gun pointing out of its tail down the line. All was well. We were free – the first time for a year.

Slowly the distance between us and the receding train increased – one hundred yards – two hundred – three hundred. I looked back at the others. They were lying motionless facing the opposite direction. Now the front of the train was coming into view as it curved round to the left. I hadn't noticed that bend in the line when I looked out of the window.

Now the whole length of the train was coming into view as it drew away across my left front and I noticed the heads of some sentries looking out of the window at the countryside. I realised our danger at once but it was too late to move. So long as the train had carried straight on, we were as safe as a house, but now that it was broadside on to us, those sentries were looking straight in our direction. I froze to the ground, while keeping my eyes glued to their heads.

Suddenly one of them jerked back inside and reappeared with a rifle. Simultaneously there was a scream of brakes as the train was brought to a standstill. I leapt to my feet, and yelled 'Quick, run for it,' and slid down the far side of the embankment, leaving my pack on the line in my hurry. Jack was close behind, carrying his pack. Philip and Mike slid down the other side of the embankment. In the same split second there was a burst of rifle fire, one shot zipping through the grass just in front of Philip's feet. Jack and I were in dead ground and could hear the shots whining over our heads.

Philip and Mike were in an impossible situation. They had not been watching the train, so, hearing my shout, they ran in the first direction that occurred to them. Now there was nothing to hide them from the train, except a ditch in which they lay, until picked up by the Germans.

Jack and I had a better run for our money. As we crouched behind the embankment, Jack asked me where my pack was. 'Up there', I said pointing to the line, 'and I'm not going to risk a bullet going up there to fetch it.' We looked round for a line of escape. The shooting had stopped but the sound of the Germans calling to each other was growing louder. With no-one in sight we climbed the barbed wire fence lining the railway and then, turning right, scrambled over a hedge into a garden. A hidden strand of wire tore our clothes but we struggled through looking back anxiously over our shoulders. In front of us was a lawn leading up to a fair sized house and, half a mile beyond and up a slight incline, there was a wood. If we could reach that wood we were safe but the Germans had realised this. Fanning out across country we could see them already barring this line of escape.

We ran across the lawn. There were no signs of life in the house and, for a moment, I contemplated breaking in and hiding there but decided against it. Skirting round the left hand side of the house we came on a woodshed stacked with a large pile of branches. 'What about hiding under there?' 'OK,' said Jack breathlessly and in we dived. We worked our way through a mass of wood to the wall and lay there panting face downwards.

Almost at once I caught the sound of running feet and shouting '*Hier, hier, sehen Sie, der Spur.*' They had found our track through the trampled grass. Next minute they were in the shed. '*Heraus,*' rang out shrill and staccato. We lay dead still, hoping we were invisible, but expecting a shot to ring out. '*Heraus oder schiessen.*' Still we lay there holding our breath. Sweat poured from me, drenching our clothes and my heart thumping so that it seemed as if it must give us away.

Then followed a crackling and crunching sound, as one of the guards climbed onto the wood stack and thrust his rifle barrel into my stomach. '*Hallo, hallo,*' he shouted, '*hire send see,*' then another

'*Heraus.*' We waited no longer but climbed out, as best we could, the rifle barrel jabbing at us all the time. By now a dozen guards had collected and, as we were marched out with our hands up, every barrel pointed at our stomachs and we imagined fingers twitching nervously on the triggers. The Germans were in an extreme state of excitement and rage and I expected one of their rifles to go off any minute.

I led the way back along the railway line to the train. Every few steps there was a thump as Jack met the full force of a rifle butt between the shoulder blades. He struggled on manfully while I was torn between my better self, telling me to let Jack go ahead thereby taking the blows upon my own back, and the cowardly instinct which stopped me.

All the train's windows were up and the German guards threatened to shoot anyone who looked out. The four of us were thrust into the guard's van and the buffeting began in earnest. An officer called Fürstenberg looked on but made no attempt to stop it. Mike came off the worst. He put his arm up in self-defence and was set upon like terriers worrying a badger. I came off the lightest perhaps because I quickly realised that any movement was sure to cause a fresh onslaught.

For an hour we were kept standing, facing the corner of the carriage, and, when at last allowed to sit down, we felt limp with exhaustion. We succeeded in hiding anything of value and then, for lack of anything better to do, I produced my 'Viceroy' razor and started shaving. The guards' attention was at once arrested. Their curiosity overcame their fury and the reminder of the journey we enjoyed in comparative comfort.

Chapter 8

Olympia

Biberach was the typical prison-camp I had pictured in peace-time – clean huts, good washing facilities – a change after the solitary pump in Posen – gravel parade and football grounds and wire everywhere. The tantalising sight of the Swiss mountains sixty kilometres away made the wire feel all the worse. A number of officers had arrived before us from Thorn and we heard the news that Germany had invaded Russia. This was greeted with extravagant enthusiasm although the early reports of German advances confirmed the confidently expressed view of the sentries that it would be all over in four weeks. Through wishful thinking, and instinctively harking back to the campaign of 1812, most of us felt convinced that Germany had overstepped it this time and we were heartened to feel that we were no longer alone in the war.

A large party of officers arrived from Greece a week later. Most of these were from the 4th Hussars but there were three from our Ranger Battalion whose experiences had a marked similarity with ours a year previously. It was the old story of the military being forced into an expedition without adequate air support by the politicians and with the inevitable result – evacuation. They had not learnt such from France.

After our attempt to escape from the train we were sentenced to four days close confinement. The cells were clean and well fitted out, but the days dragged terribly and at time I felt an overwhelming feeling of claustrophobia. I had not yet realised the cure – heavy literature and hard work. About the escape we had no regrets. We felt it was an act of God that we had been caught and nothing we could have done would have helped. But we felt self-justified and our shaming lack of initiative on the march, inertia at Laufen and bad luck at Posen were now forgotten. It was a case of better luck next time.

After only three weeks of baking hot weather at Biberach, a party consisting of all the field officers, several volunteers and those of us who had served a sentence – about a hundred in all – was ordered to prepare to move. I was not particularly sorry. Although over forty officers escaped later on, several reaching Switzerland in safety, I had a feeling that the plan I was concerned in would not succeed and in fact it did not. There were few other interests there beyond sunbathing and I would have been desperate seeing others escaping while I stayed behind. Moreover it was rumoured that we were off to Tittmönning, which sounded one of the pleasantest camps in Germany.

We made few preparations for the journey, because we imagined the Germans must have learnt from their last experience, and would guard each carriage. We travelled as far as Ulm in a railway truck resembling a train and, while changing trains here, James very cleverly stayed behind, escaped and was caught a week later on the frontier. We jolted on slowly, stopping at Munich in the evening where we had supper in a Red Cross hut. To our surprise there were no guards in the carriages and it was clear that during the night there would be a good chance to jump off the train.

Jack and I made hurried preparations and, soon after dark, our chance came as the train pulled up an incline. The guards flashed their torches out of the windows when the train was going very slowly, but when it got up to about 30 m.p.h., they retired into their carriage giving us our chance. The prospect, however, was not too encouraging. The doors being locked, one had to jump some ten feet from the window and, in order to make sure of getting clear of the train, one had to jump well out. The pitch darkness made it impossible to see where one would land or to estimate how fast the train was travelling so the chances of breaking a bone or hitting a telegraph post seemed high.

We got ready to jump from different sides of the carriage and this sort of conversation followed. 'Jack, in case we get split, I'll call out "Hulloh" and you answer "Jack – O.K. Halloh." "Like that?' 'No, sounds too public school – "Hullow" like that.' 'Hullow', 'Hullow', 'Hulloie.' 'That's better. I say, how fast is it going your side?' 'Bloody fast. What about your side?' 'Very hard to tell. Can't see a thing.' 'Christ! Did you hear that? Someone's gone from the next carriage. And another. And another. What about it?' 'Wait a second.'

It was too late; the train had breasted the rise and was now going away at a rattling pace. Ten people in other parts of the train had seized the fleeting opportunity but we had funked it and, much to the amusement of the rest of the carriage, we began excusing ourselves. To save our faces we decided to try and hide behind the lavatory door on arrival but when at 0400 hours the train drew into Tittmönning, that early morning courage, which Napoleon described as the rarest of all, failed us and we tamely submitted to being lined up on the platform while the Germans tried to make ninety officers add up to one hundred.

At the station General Fortune was taken off in a private car and, as soon as we arrived in the camp, we found an atmosphere quite different from any we had met in Germany before. Though they searched us very carefully, the Germans were astonishingly polite, an orderly carried my bags away and I was soon surrounded by many old friends. Martin was the first to meet me having already arranged for me to sleep in his room. Jack Poole came up and told me I was messing with him, Maurice Johnson, Charlie Forester, Archie Orr Ewing, Pete McCall – all those I had not seen since Laufen seemed to be there; they looked wonderfully well and in great form.

Tittmönning was an old castle of the usual German type with a courtyard, chapel and moat, standing high up on a hill. The German commandment was a gentleman of the old school and realised that, by treating British officers well, he would save himself much trouble. The atmosphere inside the camp resembled that in a London club on a Sunday afternoon. The camp was run very efficiently by Colonel Gamble and the contrast with Laufen was as great as the difference between war and peace.

The days passed quickly with most people keeping to a regular routine. At 0700 hours a party of some thirty or more would go off on parole, accompanied by two or three guards without a rifle, to a lake four miles away where we bathed and returned in time for 1100 hours '*appel*' which took about two minutes. After lunch and a siesta we would have a cup of tea and then go off, once more on parole, to a football-ground on the far side of the town. Thus physically contented we would spend the evening sipping light beer on the terrace which overlooked a lovely valley. Passing one's eye quickly over an ugly spot twenty miles away [Laufen] one could gaze at those same snow-capped mountains, wondering at their beauty as they imperceptibly changed colour with the sinking sun.

It was an ideal lotus-eaters' existence. I was happy in my mess and, for the first time, we had so many parcels that food no longer presented a problem. Once a month, a bottle of wine was issued to everyone and we forgot our few worries in a drunken orgy. All my mail which had been accumulating for four months arrived and one day at tea I was staggered to see a large pile of over sixty on my plate. I realised that this was an experience of a lifetime and sorted them before reading them carefully, after which I felt as if I had just returned from leave, with that aching homesick feeling.

During those days of make-believe, beginning as we walked through the dewy cornfields on the way to the lake where we lost ourselves in the pure physical sensation of swimming, and ending with the close smell of tobacco plants expanding in the evening dew as we chatted in the courtyard, we eased our consciences by digging tunnels which we knew were extremely unlikely ever to be finished; we were working only at the most suitable times with none but our best friends.

The war in Russia brought the Germans to the gates of Moscow, but when a German officer tried to dissuade me from sending a card to Stafford Cripps who had sent me a parcel, I scorned the idea of its not reaching him in the Russian capital. It was easy to look at the war through rose-tinted glasses.

Two good escapes took place that summer, as a result of which three officers reached the Swiss frontier where they were caught. The majority of our party, however, who had arrived full of energy and determination to get out soon succumbed to the insidious atmosphere of *'Laisser faire'*, and we took more interest in the 13th century vases and excavated human bones than in the prospect of finishing our tunnels.

The news of a move in the autumn shocked the old inhabitants to the core. Their world was to be swept away, like that of the old members of 'Arthur's' when their club was absorbed by the 'Travellers'. Endless machinations ensued. The right people had to travel in the right railway truck so that a brilliant escape could be ensured. Four of the 'leading lights' were to be bricked into a wall in the earth, known as 'Tobruk', whence they would emerge free in a week's time. The packing of our few belongings presented apparently insurmountable problems. At last we were off. The rain descended in torrents as we marched six miles to the station, dissolving our cardboard suitcases into pulp. The thrusters manoeuvred into their selected carriage, presided over by three German guards, whence they emerged after an uneventful journey at their destination, Warburg. And Martin, Charlie Hopetoun and Pat Campbell Preston, the heroes of 'Tobruk', joined us a week later after being forced to evacuate their hide owing to bad air.

Warburg brought us all down to earth with a bump. A large hutted camp on the exposed plains of Westphalia, it resembled Biberach in design, but in place of gravel we found mud and the condition of the huts and wash houses showed that it was built before the last war. Those of us who had been in Poland were much amused by the complaints of those for whom this was the first move. The whole of Laufen had arrived, their train being attached to ours en route and, while it was thrilling to meet many old friends whom we had missed for nine months, our dread at meeting the old racketeers and 'dead-beats' was lightened by our pleasure at their discomfiture. Spangenburg, another *Oflag*, had moved here including Alan Wigan 'the second richest prisoner after Hatry'. He was in great form, complaining in his old querulous tone but taking it very well. The air force was here among whom I soon discovered John Cripps who had arrived from Lubeck with the rest of his battalion and those captured in Crete. They were very hungry and John, who was soon known as 'the Lurcher', seemed still dazed by his recent experiences.

In all there were some two thousand crowded into this mud dump, but the joy at meeting so many new and old friends, and the increased vitality in the camp, soon made us prefer this discomfort to the complacent existence at Tittmönning. Jack, who had passed this very spot while escaping successfully to Holland in the last war, was worth everything to us and collected together a wonderful lot of people to share our room. Our old mess were joined by Martin, Charlie Hopetoun [later Marquis of Linglithgow, MC] and Pat Campbell-

Preston and the number was made up to about a dozen with Peter Black and Maurice Johnson.

During the first few weeks, when the rain was falling incessantly and the German organisation was proving itself miserably inadequate to cope with the problems of a camp of this size, I retired to hospital with 'flu; there I found myself next door to Pete McCall's cousin, Tony O'Reilly, of whom I quickly became very fond. He was said to be suffering from some incurable gland disease and was given five years to live but was a wonderfully brave and philosophical character.

In some ways it was a bad winter. In order to reach the dining hall we had to wade through a quarter of a mile of slush, our room was very crowded and the carbide lighting made it difficult to read in the evenings. The war news looked black. The Russians were holding on to Moscow by the skin of their teeth, the 8th Army after relieving Tobruk and reaching Benghazi had withdrawn once more.

At Christmas the Japanese entered the war and their resounding successes in the capture of Hong Kong and the sinking of our battleships were followed inevitably by the fall of Singapore. The Australians in the camp became seriously worried for the safety of their homes. We did, however, have many consolations in our narrow life. Parcels arrived as never before so we could eat our fill and ask our friends to tea. Our Christmas dinner was gargantuan and we became intoxicated with food. Through Jack's inspiration our room developed a unique spirit. Our lives centred round Jack and within those four walls, though shut up in a prison in a foreign land, we recaptured much of the sense of peace we found in the happy mess of our regiment at home.

The frost came, followed by the snow, but we had enough coal to keep the room warm and now we could get about better outside. We constructed a skating rink on a much larger scale than at Laufen, which gave us all the exercise we could want, and when snow conditions were good, we would challenge another battalion and battle was waged fast and furiously. It was a great sight to see Dougie Bader staggering forward on his false legs, preceded by a wave of skirmishers, as he led his air-boys into action.

The large numbers provided considerable acting talent, and the shows which Wally Finlayson produced and the concerts conducted by Dickie Wood were as good as any amateur performance could be.

Life became more social and, instead of seeing the same faces every day as at Tittmönning, it became an event to visit one's friends for a meal or for 'elevenses'. Gambling was very popular and reached colossal proportions. I was lucky in winning a considerable sum early on so I could continue throughout the winter without the danger of losing heavily. 'Chemmy' passed the time and provided a thrill which was otherwise impossible.

Life was not entirely taken up with trying to amuse oneself. For the first time I got down to reading and, in studying history and literature, filled a gap in my education of which I was very ashamed, and gave my mind the mental food it demanded.

From the moment of our arrival it was obvious that the camp offered great tunnelling possibilities and, although the counter measures were extremely effective, we persisted to the end giving ourselves something to do and easing our consciences. Early in the New Year Martin, Pat and I joined a large party who became engaged on a long distance job. We advanced some fifty feet and had not yet reached the wire when the thaw turned the clay into mud and the tunnel collapsed. It gave us a great interest and was the first time I had ever worked in a tunnel which reached any distance. Despite the bitter cold, it was satisfying to feel that each load of earth we removed brought us nearer freedom and, like so many others in the camp, I became very keen.

The thaw brought another diversion. Great waterways formed themselves, down which the flood water coursed and boat racing became the sport of the moment. The construction of these demanded some skill and the excitement during the races which lasted anything up to twenty minutes was intense.

The winter merged into spring, the green corn began to appear, hares played and fought within a few yards of the wire, partridges nested and hatched their coveys where we could see them clearly and bird-watching became an all-day occupation. A new energy stirred in our veins which we worked off by running round the camp in the early morning or playing football. The latter became very professional, drawing immense crowds whose enthusiasm was excited by inter-battalion rivalry and often by betting.

The camp was thinned out, all the senior officers leaving, which to our misery included Jack. He was one of the greatest characters I have ever met and became a legend to us, so that two or three years afterwards we still missed him and tried to follow his advice. Our Colonel also left but the Senior British Officer [SBO] remained. His attitude to the Germans caused much disagreement and led to considerable unrest which was relieved by lighter incidents including the display of placards demanding our rights in the Hyde Park tradition on one of the Swiss Red Cross visits. Once when the Air Force battalion was kept waiting on parade after we had been dismissed we got out the band's instruments and marched into their midst making a terrible noise but causing the desired result of dispersing their ranks. Martin who was enveloped by the French horn had considerable difficulty extricating himself when it was seized by an infuriated sentry.

As the weather improved our restlessness grew. Tunnel after tunnel was dug but all with one exception were discovered. One in which I worked under Kip Keenleyside reached ten yards beyond the wire, another in the Indians' quarters never got beyond the 'shaft' stage and a third, which Martin started in the best position of the whole camp, survived twenty-four hours.

After the disappointment of our first effort we no longer placed any great hopes of escaping by tunnelling. But we carried on partly to keep ourselves busy, partly to occupy the Germans and partly in the hope that, out of so many starters, one might finish. In the meantime we killed the monotony of our existence by reading, playing bridge and gardening. Each hut had a small plot of land, in which vegetables or flowers could be grown, and the interest and enthusiasm derived from watching the growth of a lettuce from a seedling into its full size, was out of all proportion but it made a healthy addiction to our meals.

The news of the war was not good. General Ritchie's forces had been defeated at Knightsbridge, Tobruk had fallen and the 8th Army withdrawn to El Alamein. The Russians had retired further and further towards Stalingrad and the Germans reached the heights of Mount Elbus in the Caucasus. We preferred to rub our hands with delight at the air raids. Several times planes passed over the camp, and one night I saw a bomber flash across the face of the moon – my first sight of a British plane for two years. The Germans, not appreciating our attitude to this new mode of warfare, took it out of us in a series of raids on our huts in which everything was thrown out of the windows – lockers, food, beds and crockery, under the pretext of a search.

Early in April, a plan was made for a large scale break-out of the camp, by scaling the wire. When Martin first told me of it, I thought it would entail an enormous risk and I felt doubtful if it were practicable. But the more the plan was considered the more attractive it became until we began to feel that it would be criminal not to attempt it

The time chosen was early in September, when the harvest would be ripe, the nights drawing in and the weather still hot. During the intervening months, under Tom Stallard's leadership, the preliminary experiments were carried out and the best possible apparatus designed; personnel selected for their various qualifications were trained and rehearsed over a practice course. Meanwhile conditions outside the camp deteriorated considerably. The four separate assaults, in which over a hundred officers would have taken part, were cut down to one as a result of the attachment of an enclosure to one side of the camp, extra guards patrolling the 'outfield' and the guards being equipped with torches. Moreover security within the camp was considerably tightened up by the Germans. It was finally decided to launch four ladders at one selected spot, each having a crew of ten.

Then, during the last days of August, came rumours of a move. For ten days we stood by waiting for a suitable night but the moon was unsatisfactory. Several would-be starters stood down because a party of senior officers was moved to Rotenburg. Among these was 'Jumbo' McLeod who had originally conceived the idea and was heart-broken at missing his chance. Tom, too, should have gone but sent someone in his place and spent most of the last twenty-four hours hiding under a bed and moving about outside only when disguised.

Sunday 1 September finally arrived; it was the chosen day because the moon rose about an hour after dark. I woke up with a sinking feeling in my stomach – a mixture of the dread on a morning before going back to school and the excitement before a point-to-point. It had been a strain, during the past months, having so much time to think of all the possible eventualities – when one's morale was low wishing to get out of the whole business and, when it was high, longing for the moment with all one's heart. It was a relief to know that the days of waiting were past.

All morning and afternoon I busied myself with our final preparations. Martin was working on the last minute construction of the apparatus so I packed his things as well as my own. Everything was completed except for a final reconnaissance of the ground we were to cross in the dark which we agreed to leave until after tea. We strolled out on to the 1600 hours '*appel*' trying to suppress our excitement and to appear normal. I saw a few people talking in groups who variously seemed excited, indignant or alarmed and vaguely wondered why they could not behave naturally. I soon discovered the reason. There had been an accident in the cookhouse tunnel and John Dupree had been electrocuted. Michael Borwick who was down there with him had nearly passed out trying to drag him back and Frank Weldon had eventually gone down and succeeded. We fell in for '*appel*', and waited anxiously for news. Gerry Porter went off to the hospital to help with artificial respiration followed by a padre.

During tea we heard the sad news. John had been killed instantly by the shock. This news was all the more depressing for coming on us in our highly strung condition. It was followed by exasperation when we learnt that the SBO had cancelled operations for that night on the grounds that further casualties would be bad for the morale of the camp. Our excitement which had turned to sorrow changed again to almost ungovernable fury.

Tom and Martin went off at once to try to persuade him to alter his decision. I was not entirely confident that they would succeed as he had a great reputation for 'pig-headedness'. I assumed, however, that the operation was still on and went off alone to learn our first night's march by heart and compare my maps with what was visible of the ground. Returning to the hut, I saw at once, from the feverish activity, that Tom and Martin had won their battle and that 'Olympia' [our code-word] was 'on'.

We sat down to dinner in tremendous form. Whatever my previous feelings I was completely confident now and the anxiety of the afternoon was forgotten in eager anticipation of the night that lay ahead. Gerry Porter, our PMC [President of the Mess Committee], rose to the occasion, filling us up with sausages, new potatoes, and plum pudding, and rounding off the meal with a brew of tea as strong as soup. Then, having given Archie Orr-Ewing and Peter Black our kit to take to the starting gate, we assembled in the music room informed as best we could be.

There were normally about six Germans patrolling inside the camp – keeping an eye out for illegal activities such as tunnelling. Each had to be shadowed and his position reported by torch signals to a Report Centre. Similarly the position of the German patrols outside the wire had to be reported. It was planned to divert the latter by throwing a dummy against the wire about 100 yards to the right and left of the assault point, together with a dummy ladder and a grappling hook, thrown into the wire fence and pulled vigorously by a wire from inside the camp. It was hoped thereby to make the patrols think an escape was taking place and thus delay their arrival at the assault point. Finally, when all the Germans were in 'safe' positions – and not until then – the signal had to be transmitted to the Barber's Shop [where it had been discovered, and tested some months earlier, that the perimeter lights could be fused]. Rehearsals for scaling the ladders and crossing the 10 foot gap over the two parallel wire fences were carried out over a period of several months in the Camp Music room. By day the ladder and the launching plank [for crossing the gap] were disguised as shelves on which music scores were stacked. Two wires crossed the room on one of which hung a blackboard. By 'coincidence' the height of these and the gap between them corresponded exactly with the height and the gap between the two perimeter wire fences. During rehearsals the piano and other instruments were played and, in the event of an alarm, the escapers became the choir. By the time we were ready to go each ten men crew, carrying a full pack and blindfolded [to simulate a dark night], was able to launch the ladder and the plank and to cross the wire in under 30 seconds.

The details had been worked out with incredible care and were critical to the success or failure of the operation. No-one was more aware of what failure might involve than Tom. At times, during the weeks of preparation, the responsibility had seemed almost too much for him but he was strengthened by our complete dependence on him as a leader and he carried it through without a single hitch or miscalculation.

Our own plan was very simple – to walk almost due north for two hundred miles to Lubeck, where we hoped to stow away on board a ship sailing for Sweden.

It was about 2030 hours and getting dark. The four teams were assembled with their apparatus in the two huts which ran close up to the selected spot in the wire. We blackened our faces with soot, gave our packs their final adjustment, stringing them tightly to our bodies and then each man took up his allotted position. Martin suddenly remembered he had left all his maps on his bed and I couldn't find my identity disc. Someone hurried away to fetch them.

We had drawn for positions some days ago and Martin and I had the last two places – the worst as we thought. It entailed helping the first two with the launching, then holding the apparatus for the rest of the crew before going over last. It was arranged that one non-playing member should hold down the ladder while the last man – myself – crossed the planking, but in case of the order 'Stop', he was to let go and run. It was left to our discretion as to whether we should go on over or come back; the order was to be given when the German patrols were within a certain distance of the ladders.

2045 hours at last – Zero hour. We had only to wait for the patrols to be at a certain distance from the spot, when out would go the perimeter lights, and the signal given to start. The atmosphere was unbelievably strained – tenser than anything I had ever experienced before. The hut was deathly quiet, not a light flickering and the windows all shut, making the stuffy autumn night almost unbearable. We could feel the sweat pouring in streams down our faces and under our arm-pits, and we silently cursed the number of clothes we were forced to wear.

2100 hours and still nothing happened. Had the lights failed? The awful question was in all our minds, but the anti-climax of such a possibility did not bear contemplation. We shifted our positions uneasily. A board or door creaked and everybody started then grinned self-consciously. Someone made a feeble joke, which seemed very funny. We were all feeling the strain but everyone tried to hide it.

Suddenly a whisper came from Bill Rawlings – 'the sentry has just moved up. Shouldn't be long now.' I prayed for those lights to go out with all my might. At 2110 hours they went out. 'Stand by.' I opened the door, determined that we should get a good start. Tom was already emerging from the opposite door with his apparatus. What was Bill doing? I started to move out and almost at once heard the order, 'Go.'

In complete silence the four apparatuses, each carried by four men and followed by six, moved like phantom boats out of the huts into the inky darkness and up to their allotted place on the wire. Carefully stepping over the trip wire Martin and I hoisted ours up just to the left of a telegraph pole. It was hardly in position before Steve Russell was climbing up the ladder, holding the plank out in front of his face, his body very upright supported by Maurice Johnson. With a forward thrust he sent it across and the plank clicked into the groove in the ladder – a perfect launch. Never had he done it better or quicker. At the same moment, head to tail, body after body climbed up the ladder, crawled along the plank on all fours, and swung gently through the bars at the end. The noises of the wire, rattled by the ladders under their swiftly moving human loads, seemed deafening.

Almost before Steve was over, the first shot rang out. I was prepared for that. It was probably directed at one of the diversion ladders on the flank or else an alarm signal. More shots rang out, and then cries of 'Halt! Halt!' 'Hurry up, for God's sake, hurry. Christ, what a crash as they charge through the root field.' Steve, Maurice, Pat, David Walker and Ronnie were over. On either side, like water falls, the bodies were pouring through the air and fanning out on the far side in a semi-circle.

With the escape in full flow I suddenly, if quite faintly, heard the order 'Stop.' 'He can't mean it,' I thought. 'He would have shouted much louder if he'd really meant it.' Martin never hesitated. He was already half-way up the ladder. Shots rang out more often and nearer, especially on the right. The cascade on both sides seemed to have stopped. 'Shall I? Shan't I? Shall I? Shan't I?' Perhaps the sentry was right underneath our ladder. I could see nothing. Then the thought of the humiliation on returning to the hut without Martin hit me and was followed by the thought of freedom. All these impressions flashed through my mind in a split second. The next instant I was on the ladder.

As I reached the top Martin was about to swing through the bars onto the ground. There was no-one behind me now and the whole apparatus began to slip. As I started along the planking it left the ground on the near side and Martin was just clear. The next instant it lurched forward then downwards in a nose dive. I held on tight.

As it hit the ground I crashed head first forwards, landing on my right shoulder. It was like a hunting fall when one's horse's fore-legs crumble away on landing from a big drop. Subconsciously I braced myself for the full weight of the apparatus to land on me, as if it was a horse, but the planking stuck fast in the ground. Martin helped me to my feet, whispering, 'All right?' We were off at once as hard as we could go breasting our way through the high root crop.

'Crack! Crack' went the rifles close behind, as the darkness swallowed us up. They hadn't a hope in hell now. 'Halt! Halt!' Their voices sounded plaintively in our ears. Neither their shots nor their cries bore a threat any longer. We were free. We slackened our pace and I gasped out to Martin, 'We've waited two years for this moment.'

Chapter 9

A Summer Holiday

We could faintly see the others all round us scrambling through the roots. One or two decided it was safer to keep low and started crawling on hands and knees – airmen who had never been under fire on the ground before. Martin and I made for the grassy path to our left, slipped through some paddock railings and slowed up after about two hundred yards to a steady jog. Martin was just in front and I noticed some objects spilling from the pack on his back. I caught one or two and stopped him to find that the canvas had ripped. He had to take it off and carry it in his arms like a baby for the next half hour. We went on at a good pace, trying to make out the twin church towers of Hohenwepel, but the night was black and we had to keep our direction by the stars. Occasionally the horizon in the east was lit by a flash of summer lightning like the glow from a heavy bomb.

The country alternated between roots, standing crops and stubble and was intersected by ditches. Resulting from some combination of bad eyesight in the dark and the unbalancing effect of his pack Martin fell flat on his face over every obstacle knocking all the wind out of his body and further spilling the pack. We looked back at the camp with a wonderful, but as yet unreal, feeling of freedom. The searchlights were still out, but we could see the flash of the sentries' torches and occasionally a shot rang out. There was no-one near us now but we had to persevere as we heard, or thought we heard, people behind. After about half a mile – it seemed much further – we hit the road between Hohenwepel and Menne exactly where we had hoped. Had there been a patrol on it we would have been heard when Martin took a terrible header over some wire into a ditch. We struck the footpath marked on our maps but left it after half a mile and, with

Nörde on our left, made our way across country to some woods relying almost entirely on the bright stars.

Passing down a broad ride through the woods we thought we saw a figure standing at the end. We stopped and strained our eyes but were unsure if it was a stump or a man. We decided not to risk it and retraced our steps making a small detour. Carrying on over enclosed country we were given a bad fright by the mooing of a calf which I first thought came from the dogs pursuing us. We crossed a railway at a deep cutting and a little further on met the northbound line about a mile from Nörde.

Here we had our first rest and Martin readjusted his pack binding up the rent with string. We had covered about three miles in very quick time and were short of breath especially Martin who, owing to the awkward weight of his pack and his frequent problems, had strained his heart. We did not realise this at the time but from his sudden deafness and the slowness of his reactions it was clear that something was wrong.

We carried on and shortly afterwards came to a small stream, sat down on the wooden bridge, drank thankfully, filled our water-bottles and washed the soot off our faces. It was an exquisite moment, with the moon just rising over a farmyard roof, and we revelled in the noise of the crickets, the smell of newly cut crops and the sense of our newly acquired freedom. Our senses were awakened by a new life.

Reluctantly we dragged ourselves to our feet and carried on all that night up the railway making detours around the villages of Bonenburg, Borlinghausen, and Willebadessen. We filled our pockets with pears from an orchard, green peas from a kitchen garden and ears of corn from the fields.

At one spot the railway crossed a deep valley on a viaduct and, fearing it might be guarded, we climbed down a very steep rough hill. Coming on to a shallow river, Martin took off his shoes and socks, carried our kit across, and came back to give me a pick-a-back.

Shortly afterwards as we were passing a signal box in which a light showed from an upper window a man put his head out and roared out at us. We shot down the bank on the far side going head over heels through a tangle of undergrowth and branches. So thick was it that, after trying to break through and regain the railway, we had to abandon the attempt and lay up where we were, resolving in future to keep well clear of signal boxes which showed signs of life.

It was about 0430 hours and we were just short of Neuenhause – fifteen miles from the camp. We were dog tired after the excitement and exertion of the last twenty-four hours and were soon asleep without noticing the cold. We had no difficulty in getting through the day which was typical of many subsequent ones. At about 0600 hours as it was getting light, we moved a few yards into a much better hide among beech seedlings and remained there undisturbed. We ate a bit of chocolate and an apple and slept again until 1100 hours when we cleaned ourselves up, hung our socks out to dry and inspected our feet. I was very lucky in having no blisters, thanks to my Harrods' boots, but Martin had trouble from the start. Though his feet gave him some pain they never slowed him up or affected him outwardly.

We had a big meal at midday – raisins, oatmeal, a biscuit, cheese and some chocolate. Our pockets were never empty of apples of which we ate as many as we liked. Martin had lost very little food when his pack burst so we decided to go on with twelve ounces a day for the time being. We slept in the afternoon, had a small 'tea' and studied our map carefully to learn by heart the next night's march. After writing up the log for the previous night we sat down to dinner, eating much the same as at mid-day, and then packed up our things to prepare for the night's march.

While still light we fought our way up through the jungle and waited beside the railway line for the light to fade. Then we set off down the line towards Neuenhause. We had been warned that there was a dump of sorts nearby and decided to give the village a wide berth. The railway entered a deep cutting down through which we walked until the station lights came into view. With difficulty we climbed out up an eight-foot wall but the bank was so steep and rough that we found further progress in the pitch darkness impossible. We lay down on the side of the hill to wait for the moon.

After a few minutes a train roared past; it was followed shortly by a railwayman stumbling down the line. It was lucky that we left the cutting when we did. I was soon fast asleep but Martin woke me up at midnight and by the light of the moon we clambered up the hill side without much difficulty. Entering some pine woods we spent the next two hours trying to side-track Neuenhause and regain the

Author as a schoolboy at
Horris Hill.

The author steeplechasing
at Sandown.

The author (with drawn sword) at the 1939 Sandhurst passing-out parade.

The young Lieutenant Pardoe.

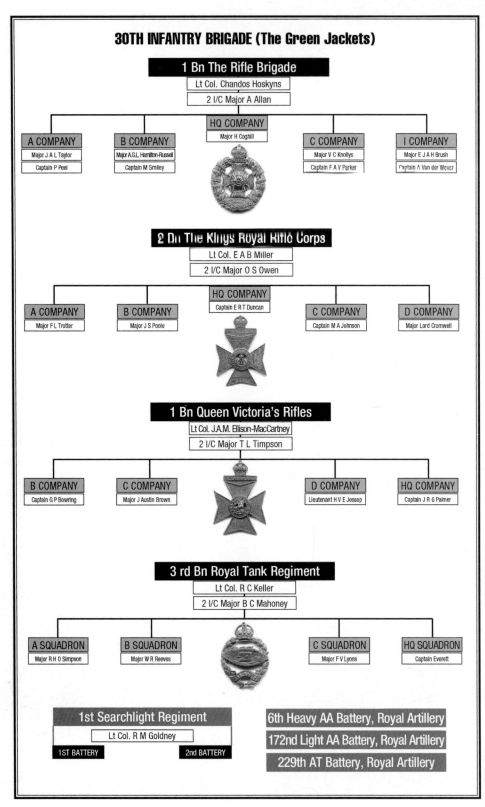

30TH INFANTRY BRIGADE (The Green Jackets)

1 Bn The Rifle Brigade
Lt Col. Chandos Hoskyns
2 I/C Major A Allan

A COMPANY	B COMPANY	HQ COMPANY	C COMPANY	I COMPANY
Major J A L Taylor	Major A.G.L. Hamilton-Russell	Major H Coghill	Major V C Knollys	Major E J A H Brush
Captain P Peel	Captain M Smiley		Captain F A V Parker	Captain A Van der Wever

2 Bn The Kings Royal Rifle Corps
Lt Col. E A B Miller
2 I/C Major O S Owen

A COMPANY	B COMPANY	HQ COMPANY	C COMPANY	D COMPANY
Major F L Trotter	Major J S Poole	Captain E R T Duncan	Captain M A Johnson	Major Lord Cromwell

1 Bn Queen Victoria's Rifles
Lt Col. J.A.M. Ellison-MacCartney
2 I/C Major T L Timpson

B COMPANY	C COMPANY	D COMPANY	HQ COMPANY
Captain G P Bowring	Major J Austin Brown	Lieutenant H V E Jessop	Captain J R G Palmer

3 rd Bn Royal Tank Regiment
Lt Col. R C Keller
2 I/C Major B C Mahoney

A SQUADRON	B SQUADRON	C SQUADRON	HQ SQUADRON
Major R H O Simpson	Major W R Reeves	Major F V Lyons	Captain Everett

1st Searchlight Regiment
Lt Col. R M Goldney

1ST BATTERY	2nd BATTERY

6th Heavy AA Battery, Royal Artillery

172nd Light AA Battery, Royal Artillery

229th AT Battery, Royal Artillery

30th Infantry Brigade Order of Battle.

Brigadier Claude Nicholson who commanded 28 Brigade with distinction during the defence of Calais. (*Jon Cooksey*)

A typical improvised barricade. (*Jon Cooksey*)

German anti-tank gun.
(*Jon Cooksey*)

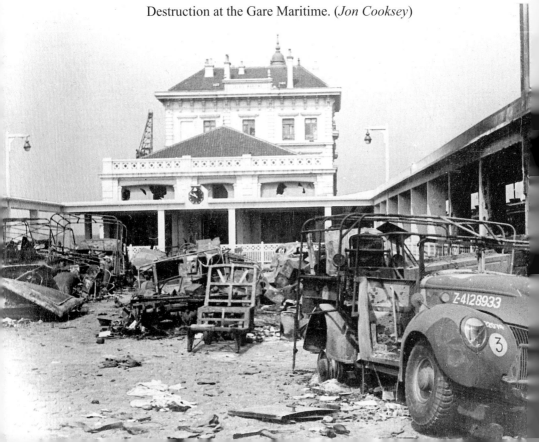

Destruction at the Gare Maritime. (*Jon Cooksey*)

Dead British soldiers at a barricade. (*Jon Cooksey*)

Allied prisoners march off to captivity. (*Jon Cooksey*)

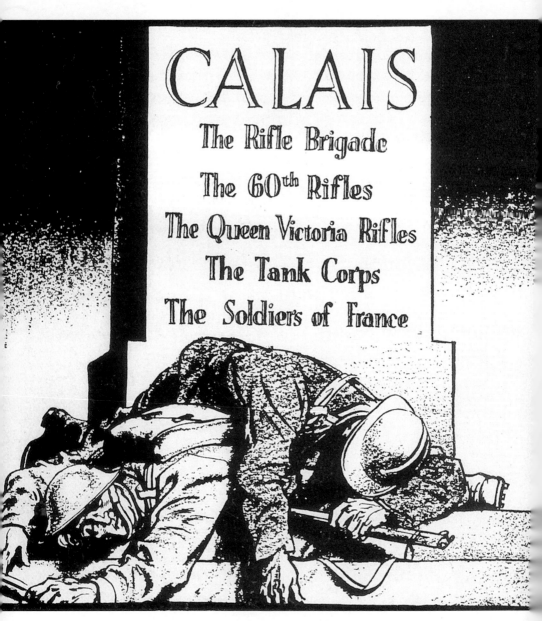

Daily Mirror cartoon evoking the admiration felt at home
for the Calais defenders. (*Jon Cooksey*)

Drawing of Laufen Camp by
Major Tim West, 5th Battalion
The Buffs, a fellow POW.

*(With kind permission
of Valentine West)*

1940 Laufen Camp Christmas Card drawn by Major Tim West.
(*With kind permission of Valentine West*)

PROGRAMME

Bobby Loder

presents

an

ALL-STAR CAST

in

McLaddin

A N D

His Wonderful Lighter

A Burlesque

Pantomime

IN TWO ACTS

Additional Dialogue JOHN LIGHTFOOT
MUSIC BY HENRY COOMBE-TENNANT, VICTOR GARRICK
AND OTHER FAMOUS COMPOSERS
DIRECTOR OF MUSIC
DONALD FRAZER

FULL THEATRE ORCHESTRA

LAUFEN ✦ CHRISTMAS ✦ 1940

Laufen Pantomine Programme designed by Major Tim West.
(*With kind permission of Valentine West*)

POWs at Posen.

Appel at Tittmoning.

Warburg. Left to right: Martin Gilliatt, Maurice Johnson, Jack Poole and the author.

Warburg: Gordon Court, Archie Orr-Ewing, Charles Clay, Jerry Porter, the author, Peter Wyatt, Charlie Forrester, Peter McCall and an orderly.

Colditz Group.
Back row: Philip Taylor, the author and Mike Scott.
Front row: Jack Hailes, Basil Brooke and Humphrey Moor.

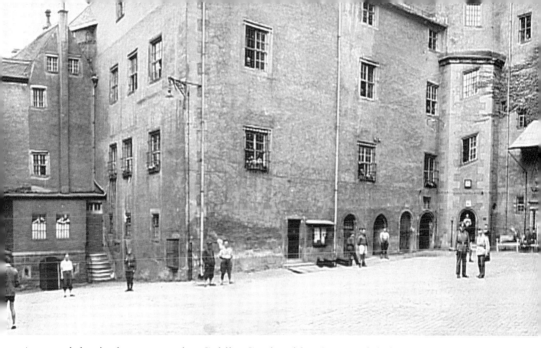

A normal day in the courtyard at Colditz Castle with POWs and their guards mingling.

Philip and his wife, Rolline.

Fishing in
Hampshire.

The author with his dog.

railway line. The tracks were sandy like those on Barossa with deep rucks made by heavy lorries. The atmosphere was very oppressive and tainted by a strong smell of petrol. At any moment we expected to run into a patrol guarding the dump and several times we passed under watch towers which luckily were unoccupied.

At last with a feeling of immense relief we emerged into open country and met the railway line. As we approached Buke station we again made a wide detour which took us into swamps where the water oozed over our boots and into woods where we stumbled over branches which made us tired and irritated. On regaining the railway line we finished well with a good march down country lanes and across stubble fields, stopping just short of Altenbecken in a young fir plantation which proved even better than our last hide. It was a disappointing night on the whole as we only covered half the distance of the previous one.

After a peaceful day we started on our third night's march intending to continue on up the railway past the junction of Altenbecken, where the Paderborn line crossed the northern one. On reaching the crest of a hill we were surprised to see the station lying below us lit up as in pre-war days. A number of wagons laden with war material were drawn up in a siding. We descended the steep slope until we came on a cutting which ran straight across our path. It was very dark and we only realised just in time that the wall of the cutting fell almost sheer down to the line. I was in favour of trying to slither down but Martin insisted on looking for a bridge which we found only fifty yards to our left. Only when we were on the bridge did I realise that an attempt to slide down the cutting would have entailed a fall of fifty feet and probably two broken necks.

Leaving the station on our left we reached a road running north which we hoped would take us back on to the line but it bent away to the east and gradually deteriorated into a foot path; at one point we found it again behind a cottage from where it led us through the pine woods and over a convenient stream where we refreshed ourselves.

The streams were fairly numerous and we never had any serious difficulty in finding water. Generally we filled up twice in the night, aiming always to end the march with a full bottle. We drank little during the day but, as soon as we were on the move, our thirst returned. We further refreshed ourselves with fruit. Trees, groaning under the weight of apples, lined the smaller roads and frequently, as we rested, apples would fall all round us as the breeze stirred their leaves.

Coming out of the wood we hit a main road which led into Horn. We walked through our first town with some trepidation. In the stillness of the night our hobnailed boots rang out on the pavements like the strokes of a blacksmith's hammer. We passed a bicyclist who took no notice of us. As we came out of the town we saw two workmen approaching. They seemed to stare hard at us but passed without a word. We were now on a first class road which led to Hameln twenty miles away. As it was after 0400 hours we branched off to the right across some fields followed by a friendly old cart horse which had been turned out to grass. After some difficulty we found an adequate hide in a beech-wood and passed an undisturbed day.

On the fourth night we decided to carry on up the main road towards Hameln side-tracking the town which, from our maps, appeared to be a considerable size. Things did not, however, go according to plan. We had finished with our large scale local area maps and were using a 'one to a million' copy, which we later discovered to be far from accurate but we couldn't blame the map for what followed.

We had paid too little attention to the route from the main road to our hide. We started out as usual at about 2100 hours and quite soon hit a country lane. It was not yet quite dark when we heard an old man with his wife and child behind us appearing to dog our steps. We decided to shake them off by turning down the first side track; this took us to a solitary cottage. The next minute excited squawks from the child told us we had walked straight up to their home. We turned round and went back past them. I muttered *'wir sind auf falschem weg gegangen'*. They stared at us unconvinced and suspicious, but to our relief they let us go in peace.

Somewhat shaken we carried on up the lane in a north-westerly direction but must have crossed the main Hameln road without realising it. For the rest of that night we were lost. Once we found ourselves heading south-west and had to retrace our footsteps half a mile. We hoped we were heading for Busingfield but the sign posts only showed Lemgo away to the left.

Later on a track took us into a farmyard. We could hear cattle moving about in their stalls and trod lightly in order not to wake the dogs. The moon was high and across our path lay what I took to be the shadow of a telegraph pole but I was mistaken. The steel tip of my boot hit a pig trough fair and square with a clang which rang out in the stillness of the night like a clarion call. The whole farmyard – dogs, cows, pigs and chickens – opened up a cacophony of alarm and we fled.

At about 0330 hours we were passing through a village when a railway worker came up from behind on his bicycle and gave us a curious look. Two hundred yards further on we came to a level crossing where we found him waiting for us with a friend. It seemed fatal to turn back so we walked on feeling anything but confident. As we drew abreast, they stared hard and one barked out, '*Wo gehen Sie hin?*' Caught on the wrong foot, I blandly answered '*hier.*' '*Wo hier, wo hier?*' they roared. '*Nach Hause,*' I answered truthfully. We hurried past while they repeated '*Wo nach Hause?*'

For the next half hour we kept glancing nervously over our shoulders. From the village the road climbed up a long steep hill with woods on either side. It was getting late so we decided to lie up just short of the crest. The woods were inhospitable with little or no undergrowth and the only cover was in a patch of seedlings twenty yards from the road. Here we spent as uncomfortable a day as I can remember and bitterly regretted our choice. People constantly passed up and down the road and we got no rest in our anxiety. We lopped off some branches which made us less conspicuous but had some bad moments expecting every dog that passed to rush in and give us away. Once a party of Germans stopped and one of them pointed at our hide. I heard one telling the others that the undergrowth must be cleared away from there and for the rest of the day we expected them to return to carry out his instructions.

A small stream trickled between us and the road, so we decided to shave. Here we discovered the only mistake in our preparations. We only had one German blade which was perfectly adequate for me but it made no impression on Martin's beard and, after some frustrating efforts, he gave it up deciding to keep the blade for a final shave near our destination. Darkness came at last to end our troubles and, reaching the top of the hill, we came on an attractive little village. People were still moving about the streets but paid no attention to us. The front door of the local pub was open giving us a glimpse of civilisation – people drinking and chatting. The smell of hot food wafted out but we had little inclination to enter.

Leaving the village we found a track running due north; it deteriorated gradually into a footpath and ended up in a pitch dark wood. The moon was not due up until 0130 hours and we nearly decided to go back; after being fortified by apples and sugar, however, we rested before plunging heroically into the undergrowth and soon emerged onto an excellent country road. After a couple of miles we came to a signpost. Martin hoisted me up to read it and there were the magic words Busingfield and Hameln pointing away to the south-east. This was exactly what we had hoped for and we threw our caps in the air for joy.

There was still better to come. The next signpost indicated that Rinteln was only just ahead; it was marked on our maps as a town of some size. We had a short rest during which we picked some potatoes and steeled ourselves for the ordeal of walking straight through. We soon entered it and came on a steel bridge which spanned the Weser. It was a broad river, perhaps four times the width of the Thames at Eton, and this seemed the only way of getting across. It was impossible to tell whether or not it was guarded so, with our hearts in our mouths, we strode out. We hardly dared glance at the river, which must have been very beautiful lit up by the moon, and we kept our eyes glued on the road expecting a sentry to step out at any minute.

All went well and we found the town as deserted as the bridge. On the far side we took a wrong turning and instead of going north found ourselves heading due east. We were talking quietly together when a German soldier overtook us noiselessly on his bicycle and, almost before we had noticed him, bent over and asked '*Feuer bitte?*' We both jumped but recovered enough to growl '*Nein! Ich habe kein Feuer.*' He rode silently into the night.

Realising we were on the wrong road we turned back and, at the cross-roads, walked into a railway yard by mistake before finally hitting the main road running north. We passed an official in some odd-looking uniform coming in to work. He stared hard at us and we decided it was high time we disappeared. After considerable difficulty, during which we nearly ran into a gamekeeper leaving his cottage, we climbed up through a very bare wood and finally settled down on the brow of a hill in a first class hide. Just below us ran an autobahn which we had not noticed on our maps. Very tired, we lay down with a feeling of deep contentment at the result of our march which had started so badly and ended so well.

This, the fifth day, we celebrated with a tin of bully beef and raw potatoes. It was a luxury we had looked forward to as the chocolate and raisin mixture which we had eaten for the last three days, although good, made us long for a change. The day was ruined for me, however, by an attack of fever, which gave me an intense thirst but no appetite. I felt tired and listless but could not sleep owing to a constricting pain over my heart.

We were undisturbed until the evening when, just as we were preparing our dinner, there was a crash in the bushes and a fox-coloured terrier went past at full gallop. Though passing within a few yards he never noticed us. We waited anxiously for the approach of his owner but he was followed only by the silence he had shattered. The autobahn, which we had hit on by accident, was marked on our maps as running north-east leaving Hanover on the right. We decided to follow it for the next twenty miles. The night very nearly started disastrously. For once the sky was overcast with clouds which obscured the North Star. After walking two hundred yards we decided to check our direction by compass and found we were going southwest – so much for our bumps of locality.

All that night we walked along the autobahn. I felt ill with a headache and a burning thirst. But quite soon we came to a little stream. I raced down the slope, burst through the bushes which lined it and gulped down the water. It was a wonderful relief but I drank too much. Dizziness came over me so that, whenever I bent down, the earth swam black before my eyes. Martin insisted on carrying my kit which was a great help and we trudged on making good progress.

The going was very easy – the road running dead straight and level, like two 'Great West Roads' running parallel with a grassy strip in between, while embankments and cuttings minimised the undulations of the country. The autobahn avoided all villages and towns, so we had little to worry about. From time to time we heard the drone of an approaching lorry and stepped off the road, usually far sooner than was necessary, and lay in the ditch until it had gone by. A bicyclist overtook us but he was evidently trespassing as much as we were for neither bicyclists nor pedestrians were allowed on those roads.

The monotony of the night was broken by an air-raid. Exploding bombs lit up the horizon far away to the north while diversion fires sprang into being much nearer. We laid up early at about 0330 hours in a young fir plantation quite close to the autobahn. It was very dense and, as we broke into it, we disturbed a roe deer which crashed through the wood startling us as much as itself. I took a couple of aspirin before going to sleep and woke up completely recovered.

We carried on up the autobahn on our seventh night's march leaving Hasta on our left, until we came to a signpost pointing to Steinude Meer. Here we turned to the left and walked some distance along the bank of the Mittellandisches Kanal passing three or four barges tied up by the towpath which showed no signs of life. After crossing the canal and a railway line we headed north leaving Wunsbach on our left. We were trying to reach a place marked Steinude on the map but which we later discovered did not exist.

We got lost in the purlieus of a village and made for some woods which turned out to be on the far side of the canal, and when at last we decided on our hide it was 0530 hours and already light. The selected spot was a thick hedgerow. We had some difficulty getting into it but, after breaking off some branches, it afforded fairly good cover.

Some cows took rather too much interest in us and threatened to demolish the hide but we were not seriously disturbed until the evening when we heard some people approaching. They started to collect wood for a bonfire and settled only ten yards from where we lay. They roamed up and down the hedge shaking our very hide in their violent efforts to break off branches and at any moment we expected to be discovered. We lay still as mice but were soon startled by the loud report of a gun as one of them fired at some pigeons. We were now in considerable danger for at the slightest movement we might have been mistaken for a rabbit with fatal results. They lit the fire and we could see them clearly – two men and a girl, sitting round eating and laughing. We spent two hours of acute suspense before they packed up and left us to breathe freely and congratulate ourselves on having survived a whole week.

We felt very pleased with ourselves. When we set out, we had few hopes of surviving for long. First we aimed at staying out beyond the next morning's '*appel*', then at outdoing Charlie Madden who had been free for five days after his escape. Now we set ourselves to beat Freddie Burnaby-Atkins who had lasted ten days.

We started off due west across country aiming to hit the railway running north from Wunsbach. We had heard the trains during the day. After about a mile we found our way barred by a canal and, seeing no bridge or ford, we skirted up its bank to the right until we came to its junction with the main canal. Exasperated, we retraced our steps over difficult country, clambering over hedges and rails, and wading through breast-high crops and reeds until, tired and dispirited, we reached the village in which we had been lost the night before. We were luckier this time, however, hitting a good road running due north parallel to the railway and lined by apple trees.

It was Sunday evening and we passed a number of people on their way home. No German can walk without talking so, to avoid a sheepish silence, I broke into a monologue of platitudes whenever a pedestrian passed within hearing. '*Es ist schon spät,*' I would say '*letzte Nacht waren wir viel fruher. Es ist ziemlich dunkel. Schade dass es keinen mond gibt,*' etc. Martin at first interspersed these remarks with '*Ach Ja*', which sounded so comic that I could barely keep a straight face. He finally compromised with '*Nein*' which sounded better if making less sense. The people took no notice of us and we gained in confidence.

Shortly after leaving the village we heard a pair of squeaky shoes coming up from behind. To avoid letting someone fall in with us we stopped, and I pretended I had a stone in my shoe. A dapper little man strutted past wearing something like our Salvation Army uniform. We followed him for about two miles until we came to the next village when he strode up to a gate where a searchlight was turned on him. The gate led into a barracks.

We were very close to daylight and hesitated for a moment as to whether we should turn back. We decided to take the risk and walked bravely on. A German NCO, unarmed as far as we could see, strolled out to stop us and we pretended to take no notice. There was a shout of '*Hallo.*' We walked on, pretending not to hear. '*Hallo! Halt.*' There was no mistaking his intention now. We stopped and I tried to look surprised. *'Was woollen Sie?'* I asked. *'Wo gehen Sie hin?'* he barked. *'Nach Hause,'* I answered truthfully as usual. He became more interested, so I said, *'Ich kann nicht wartenmuss weiter gehen,'* and we moved on.

There was a shout of *'Halt! Halt! Posten! Schiessen!'* We broke into a run and clattered away down the street. A little man coming towards us carefully got into a ditch to let us pass and then shouted louder than the rest. We went for all we were worth, expecting a shot to ring out behind, and, rounding a corner, we nipped into a garden. Lying down in some friendly cabbages we watched our pursuers go past – soldiers on bicycles, their rifles slung across their backs.

We gave them a quarter of an hour's start and then walked cautiously through the village. Whenever we heard someone approaching we hid; once a soldier questioned a woman about us within a few feet of the ditch in which we lay. We soon arrived at Neustadt, a town of some size although it was not on our map and here we took a wrong turning. After retracing our steps for about half a mile we found the right road and finished the night with a good march to a hide in a conifer wood just outside a village.

We were woken up at 0600 hours by the shrill voices of the factory girls bicycling to work. Then from another direction came the tinkle of bells and out of the misty dawn appeared two cart horses off for the day's ploughing. The farm lads sat side-ways across their broad backs while steam rose from their flanks. It was an exquisite glimpse of rural life. The day was uneventful. We washed ourselves in a deep ditch and, more refreshed than clean, started out on our ninth night's march. Passing through the village we found a number of people chatting in groups or moving about. An old man came across the road to talk to us but a firm *'Gute Nacht'* seemed to satisfy him.

We had little idea where we were. It was some time since we had seen a familiar name on a signpost, but we kept the North Star as far as possible straight ahead and, when the road curved away to the east, we turned off down a country lane. Like all other lanes this one gradually petered out and we found ourselves plunging across country. I was given a bad fright by walking straight into an electric fence. Its current, designed for cattle fencing, was weak and Martin [ex-Signals officer] insulated it with his mackintosh.

In the distance we could see a light which puzzled us for some time. Perhaps it was an illuminated building. We made for it hoping to find a road but the country was difficult and we tore ourselves and our clothes clambering over some hairy obstacles. We swore never again to leave the road for a track. It was a strong temptation when the road seemed to be taking one in the wrong direction, but it never paid. We were in the last extremes of exasperation when we hit a main road and, after passing through a village, we lay up in some young firs on the far side with no idea of our whereabouts.

Our hide was close to a farmyard and during the day some chickens and a duck came close to us, pecking about for food. We planned to trap one by laying a trail of raisins but perhaps it was lucky that we failed. We did not really need the food and the squawk of the frightened bird might well have led to our discovery. While studying our maps we noticed a place called Schwarmstedt, which both of us thought, but were not sure, we had seen marked on a signpost. If this were true we were considerably further north than we had calculated. We decided to return some three miles in order to make sure, and if our memories proved correct to take that road. This we did, finding the signpost near the place where we had joined the main road. We passed the illuminated building which turned out to be a mill, and we could hear the machinery clanking from some way off. The town of Schwarmstedt puzzled us considerably. As far as we could make out it consisted of a level-crossing and two houses, yet our map only marked the largest places. It was an enigma we never solved. A friendly little postman showed us the way at a cross-road and we carried on up one of the few first class roads marked on the map. It was cobbled and Martin suffered hell from his blistered foot preferring to walk in the deep sand of a pathway. I kept to the cobbles. We went through a town called Ahlen and, remembering that bully beef was on the menu for the following day, we filled our pocket with potatoes. They were a lucky find for the night was black as pitch.

Tuesday, 8 September we enjoyed more than any other day. We were in a perfect hide – heather to form a springy couch, young firs for protection from view and no branches overhead to keep off the sun in which we basked. We were miles from any town, and in the evening, for the first time, we lit a fire and roasted the potatoes. Our appetites had sharpened considerably since the first few days which gave the meal that quality which no well-fed stomach can appreciate.

We may have been over-cautious when lighting fires. The smoke from dry twigs was hardly visible in the dusk and, provided that the hide was secluded, there was little chance of it being noticed. We had, however, brought no tea or cocoa with us which, in the warm autumn weather, we considered an unnecessary luxury so we played for safety and, except on rare occasions, contented ourselves with cold meals.

The night's march started badly by my leaving a scarf behind at the first halt. I remembered it after we had gone on a short way, but could find it nowhere. At about 2330 hours we came into Walsrode, a town of some size. It was drizzling slightly and the streets were full of people. Here we lost ourselves completely.

First we left the town on a road which bore away due east. As we returned we blundered, first into a railway siding, then down a cul-de-sac, before at last discovering the road we had been seeking. The people we met were too concerned with reaching their homes and escaping from the rain to pay any attention to us and we felt safer in that town than almost anywhere. We finished the night with a good long march before hiding up in some beech trees on the outskirts of Visselhövede. There was little undergrowth in the wood and a heavy dew made things uncomfortable until the sun was up. We had a bad scare in the afternoon when an old woman arrived to collect fire wood. She came gradually closer to where we lay with our boots off and our belongings scattered about. Martin pretended to be asleep while I watched her, fascinated, until she was within fifteen yards. But for the branches we had lopped off to improve the hide she must have seen us but we were lucky. When she had gone and the sun was down we lit a fire and cooked some oatmeal in a bully tin. Time was making us more fastidious and less cautious. Raw oatmeal had been good enough on the first day out.

Now was the best moment of the day; the light faded and pigeons came flopping in to roost – the first we had seen in any numbers. An old cock pheasant flew up to his perch with a loud clatter and sat there calling 'cock-up, cock-up, cock-up'. It brought me straight home to evenings in Furzen Lease waiting with a gun under the tall fir trees. After the pigeons came the rooks, chattering to each other as they flew overhead with an occasional jackdaw, and then at last the thrushes went to roost 'cheep-cheeping'. An owl hooted.

We left the wood reluctantly and entered Visselhövede. Martin lit a match in the square to help me to see the signboard. A postman arrived and asked where we wanted to go. *'Nach Rotenburg,'* I said. It was a town eighteen kilometres to the north. He directed us politely without questioning why two tall strangers should want to walk so far in the middle of the night.

About two miles outside the town, we were overtaken by two policemen on bicycles. They looked suspiciously at us, stopped, and asked where we were going. I told them but they looked surprised and asked if I didn't know the road was closed. I said that I had no idea that was so and we would go back but my German aroused their suspicions. *'Sie sind Kriegagefangene,'* one of them barked. I spat in disgust and said we were workmen. He was unconvinced and things looked critical. While he was turning his bicycle around Martin and I took a sudden leap over the ditch, broke through the hedge, and ran as hard as we could go. Whistles blew, torches flashed, and we heard angry shouts as some troops turned out of their barracks nearby.

We were safe in the darkness of the open country but knew we must regain the road, sooner or later, if we were to reach Rotenburg so we made our way back through some farm buildings. As we reached the middle of the farmyard, a light swung round the corner and a bicyclist came into view. We froze where we were, beside a ridiculously small bush. The man knocked at the door of a cottage and was answered by a young girl. He asked if she had heard or seen anyone and, with more sense than most Germans, he went inside. The door closed behind him and we made good our escape. It all happened within a few yards of where we crouched.

We found our old road and later on came to a big cross roads with a pub on the green in the centre. As we looked at the signpost we were startled by a roar of abuse. A drunkard went staggering past too far gone to notice us. We carried on up the main Verden-Hamburg road and entered Rotenburg at about 0400 hours. It was the largest town we had yet come to. The street lamps were on but there was no sign of life and our footsteps echoed eerily on the deserted pavements. It was a relief to reach the open country again and we laid up on the far side among some beech trees beside a railway line. It was a lovely day and the sparrows hopped about on the twigs above our heads; in the evening a leveret came to within a few feet of us and actually started nibbling at our hide. We were at one with nature. The wild birds had taken us into their confidence and we shared their fears and instincts in our common avoidance of mankind.

With some misgivings we prepared ourselves for the thirteenth night's march. We were now travelling very light having completed three-quarters of the journey. Each night we had less food to carry and, although experience gave us confidence, the very act of packing and the thought of the coming march gave me a hollow sinking feeling in the pit of my stomach. Tonight it seemed worse than before. Soon after starting we came to a river where we both had a good wash and drink and filled up our bottles. Back on the road again we were passed by several bicyclists one of whom – I may have imagined this since – looked back at us suspiciously.

We had slightly modified our plan. It seemed that, as Hamburg was directly on our road to Lubeck, it would be worth looking in there on the chance of finding some Swedish shipping. We hoped to reach the banks of the Elbe after another two nights. There I was to clean myself up and enter the town by day to explore possibilities and return to Martin's hide with what news I could pick up. If there was no sign of Swedish shipping we would carry on up the autobahn and aim to reach Lubeck on the nineteenth night. This would leave us with a few days' reserve of food, in case we had to wait.

We were discussing these plans and almost visualising our arrival home when, without warning, military policemen leapt from the ditch on either side of the road. A bright torch blinded us, a revolver was thrust in our ribs, and they alternately rained blows on our faces and turned our pockets out yelling *'Hände Hoch! Hände Hoch!'* We were taken completely by surprise. It seemed on the spur of the moment that they must know who we were and, in reply to their questions, we admitted that we were British. Their attitude changed immediately and we were conducted into the village of Scheesel.

So our fortnight's freedom came to an end. We had embarked on the operation feeling that we had less than even chances of getting clear of the camp and, once out, my own opinion was that the odds were high against our reaching Lubeck – as for reaching England, well, that sort of thing just did not happen to oneself. But the risks we were taking seemed amply justified by the chance of even a taste of freedom and our hopes and expectations were realised.

The feeling of freedom was at first unreal. Two and a half years behind the wire had made us forget what it was to be one's own master yet we had thought about it so much that it seemed that we were in a life of dreamland. At any moment we might wake up and find ourselves back in the hut at Warburg. We never ceased to extract the maximum from every moment of the day and night knowing that at any time our adventure might end abruptly. But after a time we began to feel we had been free for ages and looked back on our life in prison with only the more pleasant recollections – laughing at the daily chores and squabbles which at the time had seemed so unbearable.

During the beautiful nights, we revelled in things that normally pass unnoticed – the smells of crops moistened by the dew and the farmyards, the ceaseless chirruping of the crickets, the hooting of the owls and the barking of dogs. They all recalled the days of peace in England.

The stars came to take the place of the countryside for showing us the way, and we got to know the main constellations intimately. The Great Bear started high up in the sky in a horizontal position while, as the night wore on, it sank lower and lower. Orion and the Pleiades were our friends, for they rose later in the east to tell us that our night's march was nearly over. The moon was very kind to us. On the first night it allowed us to escape in inky darkness and rose an hour later to guide us across the fields. On each subsequent night it rose three-quarters of an hour later and so, after a week, it left us for good. Although we missed its light when searching for a hide we felt safer in the dark – particularly on the two occasions when we were chased.

The days I enjoyed almost more than the nights; we slept well for seven or eight hours and, during the remainder, we would rest contentedly; as the sun broke through the leaves of the trees to dry and warm us we were never too hot nor were we troubled by mosquitoes. We had little inclination to read.

Partly owing to the wonderful weather and partly to our preparations and training, our health was good throughout. Other than the occasions I have mentioned we felt at the top of our form and were no wearier after the twelfth night's march than after the first. Looking back on the whole expedition neither of us had a regret concerning our preparations, plan, or anything that subsequently happened and we felt grateful that at last, by great good fortune, we had managed to survive a fortnight as enjoyable as any we had known in our lives.

Chapter 10

A Long Weekend

At Scheesel we were taken into the local hotel where an interpreter was sent for. He was a most un-German type and, although he had just been dragged out of bed, greeted us with 'Well, gentlemen, I must say you are sports!' While the two policemen sat glaring in the corner, he set us down to a meal of cold sausage and beer and told us of his life in West Africa. He had been interned by the British in the last war and arrested by the French a week before the outbreak of this one. He was to have been repatriated for old age but he was taken off the ship in Oran and worked for several months in a chain gang in the Atlas Mountains until released after the French Armistice. He said that, given the choice, he would prefer four-and-a-half years in a British internment camp to the months in the Atlas Mountains.

Almost our first question to him was to ask if Stalingrad had fallen – when we escaped the German press had been treating this as a matter of days. The answer was 'probably to-morrow'. We avoided further discussion on the war or politics which, even with the most reasonable Germans, invariably led to heated argument.

We spent the night in the local cell which had no window, stank of urine and was furnished with one small bed with a leg missing. Next day, 12 September, we left by train for Bremen. We kept our eyes open for air-raid damage but were disappointed to find the station quite untouched. We never got a chance to see the docks but, apart from a few roofless houses, the main town seemed to have come off lightly. The morale of the people appeared normal. The men were in every conceivable kind of uniform and the women were smart and neat even if their clothes gave the impression that they would dissolve immediately if exposed to a thunderstorm.

We were taken to Gestapo headquarters which we entered with

some trepidation but found ourselves being cross-questioned, not by the ruthless type we had expected, but by the most courteous civilians who took the maximum trouble in doing the minimum of work. We spent the rest of the day together in a cell with a Czech on one side of us and a Polish girl on the other.

We were called for in the evening by a Marine NCO and a sentry and taken by rail to Tarmstedt, thirty miles away. They were uncongenial companions; the NCO was old, ugly and talked as if he had a plum in his mouth and his awkward young colleague was proud of his schoolboy English in which he tried to explain that it was a matter of indifference to him whether we arrived alive or dead. At the far end, we had a walk of three miles to a camp called 'Marlag und Milag Nord'. Although accustomed to walking up to twenty-nine miles a night for the last fortnight the reaction after being caught had physically prostrated us and we were quite exhausted on arrival. In the guard room we were exasperated by a facetious conversation with two German naval officers while awaiting the security officer who carried out a very thorough and intimate search of our clothes and bodies.

We spent three days in the Marlag, sleeping two of the nights on hard boards. We were very weak. Apart from the effort of walking two hundred miles, the mental strain of having to think what to say or do at every moment of the day and night under every conceivable situation had taxed our nervous reserves to the full; the accumulated effect of two-and-a-half years on tinned food had also left its mark. While the goal of freedom was still in sight we had enjoyed the necessary spur to activity, but the collapse of our hopes had left us flat. Under normal conditions we should have had no difficulty in breaking out of those cells, but now the necessary energy simply was not there.

Our third evening was brightened by the arrival of a naval officer, Tommy Catlow, who had escaped from the Marlag by a tunnel. He had been forced to leave all his food behind, but had nevertheless succeeded in reaching Denmark, living for nearly a week on raw turnips. He told us he had met Chan Blair in Gibraltar the previous summer on his way back to England after escaping from Biberach.

The next day I heard a tap on the window and looked out to see the grinning face of a black man who asked me if there was anything

I wanted. I told him eggs. 'Yeah, Sah,' he said, 'I'll sure go squeeze a hen'. He may have but, at that moment, two Germans arrived to take us back to Warburg. We were hustled into a lorry where I saw a woman sitting on a sack of potatoes. Thinking she was a German, I was making for the other side of the lorry when I was startled by the words, 'Say, won't you sit down here!' She had lived for seventeen years in Panama but, being a German by birth, had been interned on the outbreak of war. After several months behind barbed wire, guarded by machine guns, she and her son had been exchanged via Sweden. Her husband was still there and the look of suffering in her face was more eloquent than any words describing her experiences.

Our journey back to Warburg was uneventful. While stopping in Bremen for some soup we had an amusing conversation with some Russian troops even if few of us understood a word the other was saying. We had a few hours rest on the hard floor at Zoest and, during the last stage of our journey from Altenbecken to Menne, we enjoyed a view of the country over which we had travelled on our first two nights of freedom.

We walked across the fields to the camp on a lovely autumn morning thinking of the partridges which we should have been shooting at home. We were cross questioned again by the security officer Rademacher, who was in one of his good moods. He showed us a set of photographs of the launching apparatus taken on the day after the escape and he offered them to me on condition I told him what the grappling irons were used for. He ordered his interpreter Bach to show us over his museum of escaping kit but the latter, as soon as Rademacher was gone, searched us and left us to shiver in our shirt sleeves for the remainder of the day and night in the local cells.

There we met Tom Stallard, who had been caught, after a fortnight, on the Dutch frontier. He told us that twenty-nine had succeeded in escaping of whom all but Henry Coombe-Tennant, Rupert Fuller, and Albert Ackwright had been recaptured. These three eventually succeeded in reaching England in a fitting conclusion to one of the most brilliantly planned and executed escapes of the war.

The camp was deserted, the last party having moved to Eichstätt in Bavaria, two days after we had left. Thither we followed them, arriving after an uncomfortable journey, in the early dawn. We sauntered through the town which looked most attractive and on our way out to the camp we passed a circus. The sight of an elephant looking out of the morning mists shook us considerably. On arrival we were clamped into the cells and underwent ten days close arrest.

Eichstätt was a large camp composed partly of brick buildings and partly of huts. The grounds were nearly as large as those of Warburg and allowed ample room for a football field, hockey pitch, tennis courts and a vegetable garden. Along one side ran the Altmühl, a shallow sluggish river, but the view was restricted by the hills which rose steeply from the valley in which the camp lay. The German commandant was a short, stocky, fanatical Nazi with whose passionate outbursts we soon became familiar. There were over two thousand officers in the camp including many Canadians who had been recently captured at Dieppe.

We had been away from our friends for a month, and on our return we had a great reunion. They were longing to hear about our recent experiences and we were no less eager to recount them. We were sorry to find our old mess had been split; those who had a clean conduct sheet being in the huts, known as the Garden City, and the rest in one of the brick buildings. Martin and I were taken pity on by Mike Grissell, who asked us to join his mess with Brocky Mitten, Joe Hume, Squeak Wijk, John de Moraville and Geoffrey Bowring. This suited us very well and despite some discomforts we got through the next few months reasonably well.

Soon after our arrival, the Canadians were called out on parade one morning and, with no explanation from the Germans, they were taken off to an old schloss four miles away. Precautions were taken by the Germans to prevent any incidents by letting down the flaps of the sentry posts which exposed a number of machine guns. The atmosphere in the camp was tense. It was worse at the schloss; the Canadians had no idea why they were being taken away and, as officers were led away in couples, their fate must have seemed most ominous.

Later in the day we learnt that, as a result of the alleged hand-cuffing of German prisoners at Dieppe and during a Commando raid on Sark, the Canadians were to be handcuffed until the German government received a satisfactory British assurance that this practice would cease. The British reply was to handcuff a similar number of German prisoners which led inevitably to German counter reprisals. With as little warning as before the Germans marched off the last ten files from each company and the whole of our mess, except for Squeak and John, found ourselves in chains.

It was at first an unpleasant and irksome experience. The handcuffs were released at night, and for our more intimate toilet activities, but the effect over a period caused considerable nervous strain not to mention the worry to our families at home. After a few weeks many including Martin and myself went sick and were exchanged for others. Although conditions were subsequently relaxed over three hundred officers remained handcuffed for more than a year.

The winter was the usual prison mixture of discomfort and compensations. On the black side was the overcrowded and smoky atmosphere of our quarters from which we emerged only to sink inches deep into mud. The light was bad and the carbide lamp quite inadequate for reading so we resorted to chess and similar games to while away the long winter evenings.

But the war was going far better now that the offensive had been finally passed over to the Allies. The Germans, after being trapped in Stalingrad, were falling back at a pace which satisfied the most ardent optimists, while in North Africa the Battle of El Alamein had been won, the Americans had landed and the two forces were advancing rapidly to form a cordon round the retreating Germans trapped in Tunisia.

Food parcels were plentiful and the arrival of the frost once more gave us an opportunity to work off our surplus energy. A first class ice rink was constructed on which we played hockey as long as the hard weather lasted and for the first time in my life I tried to ski. John Cripps coached me on the three short slopes; two of these commanded the respect of the most professional performers. It was a thrill which I resolved to repeat after the war under better circumstances.

The winter was broken up for me by two spells of about a fortnight in the cells for old offences committed at Warburg. They were welcome as changes from the humdrum everyday life and I enjoyed the solitude which gave opportunities for reading and contemplation impossible in the more normal crowded circumstances.

The inevitable problem of how to get out of the camp had confronted us on arrival and seemed even harder to tackle than at Warburg. Anything on the lines of 'Olympia' was out of the question given the presence of two separate wire fences; tunnelling was evidently a hard proposition owing to the rocky soil. It was eventually decided that one tunnel should be constructed starting from the lavatory in one of the brick blocks, running under the main road and coming out on the hillside considerably higher up. This would entail a straight run for about forty feet, followed by a fairly steep climb for seventy feet, with the real possibility of hitting impenetrable rock in the later stages.

It was with little or no enthusiasm that Martin and I started work. After the glamour of 'Olympia' it seemed a sordid come-down to start at the very beginning of what must be a long and difficult job. After six consecutive failures we had few illusions as to the chance of success and remembered only too well the hours of squalor and boredom involved.

But digging seemed the only way out and had the advantage of requiring little imagination and entailing the minimum of risks. Moreover in the emptiness of life any work was better than none and the slightest chance of freedom in the most remote future was better than having no straw at which to clutch. The first stone was turned about Christmas time and the first six weeks were taken up with work on the 'base'. Then things fairly got going and, by the time I went into the cells, we were averaging a yard a day. But once under the road, the pace slowed down, until progress in the face of hard rock seemed negligible. A variety of technical difficulties had to be overcome and it was not until the beginning of May that, thanks to some brilliant work by Frank Weldon and Jock Hamilton-Baillie and a fair amount of luck, the tunnel was finally completed.

All was now ready. We had completed our own preparations, collecting food and equipment, making clothes and packs, deciding on our route and copying out the necessary maps. Our plan was to travel south in the same manner as before and, crossing the Alps by the Fern Pass, to approach the Swiss frontier via the Inn Valley, close to the Italian Frontier. The distance was about one hundred and sixty miles which we knew from experience to be no difficulty. The most dangerous parts of the journey would probably be the crossing of the

Danube, which flowed across our route only twenty miles from the camp, and the actual approach to the frontier.

It was decided to wait for a suitably rough night which, after about ten days, we thought had arrived. There were over thirty of us, who had worked from the beginning, and another thirty who had helped dispose of the earth, so that, together with a few 'honorary members', some sixty-five officers were lined up for the start. At the last minute the wind dropped and the operation was called off. The next day a most unpleasant and mysterious incident came to light.

Two notes were discovered, pinned to a lavatory door and signed by a 'well-wisher', who warned us that the Germans were in full possession of all details of the tunnel, down to the actual place where it started. The writer added that sentries were placed on the hillside every night, with orders to shoot on sight. Every endeavour was made to discover the author of the note, whether German or English, as also to find out whether the Germans were in fact taking the precautions which were alleged. No clue was discovered and, apart from what might have been a routine inspection of the lavatory during one morning and the spotting of a sentry lying in some bushes on the hillside on another afternoon, they gave no indication of knowing its existence.

The operation, which had been postponed, was once more put on for the most suitable night and the strictest precautions observed to maintain absolute secrecy. Every day the sun blazed down from a cloudless sky; in the early morning I would check if there were any change in the weather then run round the camp two or three times and do some PT under the trees by the river. Most days I put the whole operation out of my mind; it was my way to keep fit and avoid becoming a nervous wreck.

The rest of the camp carried on their usual activities. There were good facilities for sport, games of tennis and hockey being played all day. The cricket season opened with the arrival of some matting and nets and we spent some delicious hours lying under the trees hearing the nostalgic and unique sound of bat on ball. Another favourite occupation was bird watching and, from the earliest hours in the morning until dusk, solitary figures were seen gazing up at a nest and noting down every activity of the parent birds. Every evening these notes would be collected and published in weekly reports. There was no privacy at Eichstätt – not even for birds.

3 June was just such a day as we had had for the last month, warm and sunny, with a nice breeze which invariably fell to a perfect calm about supper time. It was decided to celebrate the King's birthday with athletics and, to our disgust, Jack Higgins invited the commandant and his staff to witness this very British exhibition. After tea we went over to the cricket net to get our eye in for the morrow's match when OEs all over the world would be celebrating 'the 4th of June'. The weather promised to hold fair but it was the last night for a considerable time there would be no moon so we knew that, given the least excuse, the powers that be would let us go.

The sports were over, the Highlanders had 'beat the retreat' and Jack had taken the salute. As we strolled back to supper and took a last look at the sky, a dark cloud far away in the west raised our hopes of a stormy night. When we came out for the 2030 hours parade the cloud was much nearer and the leaves were rustling. A tingle of excitement ran coursing through my veins. Martin, who was in the know, caught my eye and nodded. It was on.

As we walked back to the hut Mike Grissell, one of the non-starting officials, came stumbling up looking grim as thunder and pregnant with information. Out of the side of his mouth in a tense whisper he hissed 'OK' and we just burst out laughing. Mike hated the whole business on the nicest possible grounds. My immediate action was to do a roar. Our preparations were a matter of a few minutes and we said goodbye to our room.

They were very charming, thrilled and sympathetic, but could not disguise the fact that they expected us back the next day. We then looked in on Everard Radcliffe and Maurice Johnson. There were signs of panic in the room, as John Arundel kept losing things as quickly as they were found. Everard was charming, full of enthusiasm and good wishes, and Maurice curt as ever – perhaps a little jealous.

Up in the brick block things were going on quietly and efficiently according to plan. Frank and H-B were just going down the tunnel, when we looked into Pat's room to say goodbye to the few who were not coming with us. Then we moved into the assembly room known as 'Henry'. It was very exciting. We took up our places, each in the order we had drawn, like horses at the start of a race, with feelings very similar to those of their jockeys. Martin and I were numbered 22 and 23. It was very quiet.

The wind had dropped completely and only the chirping of the crickets on the hillside broke the stillness of the evening. The two Charlies [Hopetoun and Forester] were sitting opposite us and we chatted in whispers. They seemed very keyed up for this was to be their first 'outing'. We felt very old stagers but I expect we sounded equally tense. The places we had drawn seemed bad enough but they were in the 50s and could not hope to get out until about 0300 hours. It would be a trying ordeal.

At about 2130 hours the first six crawled out silently, one behind the other, and we moved up to fill their places. No orders were given. Everyone knew his part. A long wait followed, while the delicate work of 'breaking the surface' went on below. I made myself more comfortable and closed my eyes. Perhaps half an hour dragged by. They were taking a long time. Anxious doubts began to flood my mind. What could be happening? Why were they taking so long? At this rate we would be lucky if we got out by daybreak. At the back of our mind lay the expectation of a rifle shot ringing out at any moment.

At last there was a movement – 'Number 10 please'. We all moved up one. 'Number 11'. It was working. We pictured the first few already crawling on hands and knees up the hillside. Regularly we moved on up until it came to Martin's turn. He disappeared, and I moved up to the 'P' bucket. Never was I more glad of it. Then 'Number 23'.

Trembling with excitement, my Gebirgsjaeger cap pulled well down over my face, and pack slung across my shoulder, I crept to the top of the staircase. 'Cigarette?' There was the gaunt figure of John Arundell. He was obviously in his element, and could hardly suppress his excitement. 'The crickets are making a hell of a noise', he whispered, 'it's going like clockwork – shame to take the money.' Cecil was standing in his dressing-gown at his bedroom door. 'My dear Phil, you look charming,' he whispered. Of all the fatuous remarks, I thought then, realising that he meant well and was trying to break the nervous strain, I grinned gratefully. Silently I slipped down the stairs, and passed Freddie Burnaby-Atkins, blinking short-sightedly. 'Good luck!' 'Thanks.'

Tony Holt was at the tunnel entrance officiating. 'Good luck, Phil,' he whispered. 'It's an absolute push over. You can't help making it. Everything's going like clock-work. Never been more confident in my life.' They were exactly the same words. I let go of my pack which slid down the shoot, and followed on my back, feet first. There at the base of the tunnel, in the dim light of a flickering carbide lamp crouched Hecky [Hector Christie] just like a huge dog. He adjusted the pack which was tied to my waist with string. I wished he was coming too.

I started crawling up the groove. Seeing no-one in front I went as fast as I could, catching up Martin at the foot of the slope, where I had time for a short breather. The air was very bad with the same dank smell of wet clothes, wet boards and wet soil mixed with carbide fumes. I breathed quickly but could not satisfy my lungs. I had only known it as bad as this once before – in Kip Keenleyside's tunnel at Warburg.

Now we were moving on again up the slope. The ceiling was lower here and I had to keep down, almost on my back, propelling myself with one elbow and one leg. At the next pause, I glanced forward at Martin and saw a large white card marked '22' attached to his pack. I wormed my way up to take it off and he grinned back. I could see he was also having difficulty with his breathing.

On we went, safely under a large slab of rock known as 'the coffin', past a flickering lamp, through an excavation where we had particular trouble, known as 'Alladin's Cave', on to Piccadilly Circus where the tunnel forked. The worst was over. Very faintly I felt a breath of cool air, coming from the outside. It was just as well. Hampered by my heavy clothes and the boots in my greatcoat pocket, I was feeling exhausted. Sweat was streaming from every pore in my body.

Jack Hailes was in the 'Side Street' doing something to Martin's pack. He was breathing heavily and looked very exhausted. Martin moved on, and I heaved my body up over a ledge and – SNAP! The cord attached to my pack had broken. I slipped back and managed to draw the pack up towards me with my feet. I tied a knot in the string and moved up again, just as Martin stepped from the tunnel into the dark void of the outside world. I moved up into his place and – SNAP! It had gone again. Almost simultaneously Bertie, who was squatting by the exit, put his hand on my shoulder, motioning me to stay still. We waited tensely and heard the 'clip clop' of hobnailed boots coming up the road.

Nearer and nearer they came until they seemed to be within a foot of the hole, where they stopped. I hardly dared to breathe. Lying flat on the floor of the tunnel and looking up at the stars above, I waited for a shout or a rifle shot. Was it my imagination or could I actually hear him breathing?

For a long time there was complete silence – silence too from the tunnel stretching away below me. The others had seen the red light and were lying motionless. Even the heavy panting, which had seemed deafening before, had ceased. I lay there thinking of Martin. If he was only just out of the hole the sentry must spot him. 'Please God, don't let him shoot.'

Ten minutes – a quarter of an hour went by and there was no move. I began to feel more confident. Lying there with the open air above, I had been able to fill my lungs and was beginning to breathe more normally. Then to my relief I heard the footsteps move on. Bertie raised himself cautiously, peered out and nodded to me. It was all clear. Suddenly I remembered my pack and wondered how the hell I was to get hold of it. There was no room to move round and my feet could not get a grip on it. I could not face crawling back and so made signs to Jack Hailes and to Kip who was immediately behind me peering up like an otter out of the depths below. Between them they managed to push the pack forward until I could reach it.

Stretching up from my cramped position, I slung it over my right shoulder and looked outside. It was like looking into another world. The palings which lined the road were within a foot of me, and seemed brightly illuminated. So did the grass all around. For a moment I thought the searchlight from the sentry box a hundred yards up the road must be shining on me, but then I realized that it was the white building which reflected the perimeter lights on to the hillside. Coming out of the utter darkness of the underworld, it seemed quite bright where in reality there was only the dimmest reflection.

Bertie's hand on my shoulder roused me from my reverie as he gently urged me out. It seemed a big step to take. Inside the tunnel lay comparative safety but, once out on the hillside, one was at the mercy of the searchlights and machine guns. I looked round once more but there was no sign of life. Raising my right leg out of the hole I gave a jump and hit the open. The nightmare was passed and the dream of freedom lay ahead.

On hands and knees I crawled up a pathway made by twenty other bodies through the long grass towards the fence ten yards away. It seemed as if I was making a terrible noise, for the night was very still. I must have strayed from the track, for I missed the hole under the fence, but next minute I heard a low whistle from Martin. He had been waiting just on the far side all the time and he helped me under. We started up the hill on our hands and knees.

It was very steep and we soon realised we could move more quietly and quickly on our feet. We scrambled up by bounds, resting now and then to regain our breath, or freezing to the ground when the searchlights swept the slope. At last, after crossing an exposed stretch we reached the top and sat down behind the cover of a hedge with an immense feeling of relief. We gloated over the camp slumbering unconscious below.

Someone disturbed the dogs, kennelled near the Garden City, and they all started barking. We put on our packs, took a triumphant look behind us and made off along the crest of the hill due east. There was no moon to light our path and every bush looked like a crouching sentry. Once or twice we bore too far round to the right, and found ourselves overlooking the Eichstätt-Pfunz road. After half a mile we rediscovered our right track and, after several falls, reached the bottom of the precipitous slope with our ankles still intact. A farm track led us up to the main road which we crossed and, following a footpath, we made our way between cornfields to the river bank exactly where we had intended. We had performed a complete semi-circle and the camp still looked very close. The searchlights periodically swept round in our direction. Each time we fell flat on our faces, getting up feeling rather ashamed. We knew we were at least half a mile beyond their effective range but they still seemed unpleasantly bright.

So far we had heard no shots or sounds of shouting, or anything to make us think the alarm had been given. We took off our greatcoats and trousers and holding these in our arms we waded across the river in our gym shoes. It was very shallow, the water scarcely reaching above our knees. On the far bank we set about dressing, which took some time. As soon as our dry socks, trousers and boots were on, we remembered that we had not filled the water bottle. The bank was too steep to allow us to do this without getting wet, so we started off with no water trusting we would reach the Nemenfels brook before dawn. We climbed up the steep slope through a mass of tangled branches and undergrowth, crossed a railway and reached the road. At the cross-roads we took what we hoped was our last look at the camp, glanced at our watches and, at 0100 hours, we set off for Switzerland along the Eichst☐tt-Neuburg road.

Climbing uphill through the pine woods, we left the valley behind, and came out into open country where large flat fields of standing corn were interspersed with fir woods. We kept glancing back over our shoulders in case the alarm had been given and patrols sent out, but hardly saw a soul all night. A gentle breeze was rustling the leaves of the trees, and we wondered whether it would reach the valley and help cover the noise of those following us.

The first village we came to was Adelschlag – a typical collection of farm buildings. No-one was about but every dog was waiting ready to bark at us. On the far side, we came quite suddenly on the lights of a level crossing. They startled us until we made out what they were. The gate-keeper's light was burning and we saw him clearly in his room, as we clattered past in our hobnailed boots, but he took no notice. A few miles on we passed through a similar village called Mochenlobe which was equally deserted and at about 0230 hours we reached Nassenfels. We had meant to side-track the village, but missed the turning and had to walk through the streets. On the far side we found the brook exactly where we expected and, leaving the road, we clambered over some railings and flopped down to rest in the long dewy grass. We had been going hard for nearly three hours without a halt, and had put about eight miles between us and the camp, so we were not feeling too fresh. The half hour in the tunnel followed by the steep climb had been especially exhausting. Martin filled the water bottle using my flask and we had a delicious long drink. It was a lovely night, made beautiful by the music of the stream, the splash of a water rat, and the hooting of an owl. Everything seemed too good to be true.

After ten minutes we forced ourselves to face the road once more. First light was beginning to appear as we carried on down the Neuburg Road. Almost all the local Bavarians were Catholics and we passed several crucifixes by the wayside. It gave us a sense of awe suddenly to come upon a cross from which the realistically sculptured figure of Christ was hanging, against a background of heath and a cloudy sky, lit by the faintly greying dawn.

We turned off the main road down a Roman road, which led us after two or three miles into a village called Attenfield. We had meant to skirt the village but it is very easy to make false decisions at the end of a long and tiring night's march. We got involved in the back-streets and farmyards where lights were beginning to show, cocks were crowing and dogs barking. It was almost daybreak before we extricated ourselves and hurried across country to a wood close by which proved an ideal hide. Before going to ground we took a bearing on the village and found we were to the north-west of it instead of the south-west which we had intended. We had badly missed our old friend the North Star.

We got little sleep that day. We had sweated so much, especially during the first part of the night, so our clothes were wet through and uncomfortable. A light rain fell intermittently which was tiresome and prevented us from drying out but we were perfectly happy. We compared our sensations on this trip with those on our last and felt almost as if this were a continuation of our journey up to Lubeck. The last nine months at Eichstätt, which had seemed to pass so slowly and monotonously, now faded into the background – an obscure interlude in one long vital adventure.

There were, however, some differences. We missed the novelty of being out for the first time; I could never repeat that unique experience as after it one knows what to expect. The season also made the country different. There were no apples with which to fill our pockets, no green peas or ears of corn, and potatoes were as yet the size of marbles. The crops were remarkably advanced for the time of year; we passed through several fields in which they came well above our heads but none were ripe.

We spent the day in much the same way as on our last trip. Our food was slightly different and for breakfast we enjoyed a mouthful or two of oatmeal cake. We much enjoyed the chocolate we had melted down with raisins and the cheese was all the better for having had months in which to mature, but the big excitement was the brew of tea. We had constructed a type of smokeless heater which was said to bring a biscuit-tin of water to the boil in about ten minutes. It was an intricate operation and we had just discovered how to get the most flame and the least smoke when one of us tipped the whole machine over. We had to start again and this time we were completely successful. It did not matter that the Klim milk powder had gone sour after five weeks' exposure or that the tin burnt our lips. It was one of the best drinks I have ever enjoyed and made our spirits soar and our stomachs relax. We settled down to an afternoon's rest completely satisfied.

After ten, we wrote up the 'log' as before and learnt by heart the route for the night's march. Then we laid the table-cloth [my red handkerchief] and served up dinner in style. This time we had no disasters with the brew.

As the light faded we packed our belongings and moved to the edge of the wood, where we ran straight into a large flock of sheep. They scampered off, and huddled together facing us, but their master and his dog were some way off and took no notice. We made a considerable detour round them before setting off almost due south across the fields at 10.15pm. Behind our left shoulder Attenfeld was just visible in the gathering dusk.

Our plan was to carry on down the Roman road, through Giotlhausen, to a crossroads two miles short of Steppeberg. There we would turn left and look for boats along the bank of the Danube as far as Steppeberg where a small tributary flowed in from the north-west. We would carry on our search up this stream as far as a village called Rennetshofen and, if we failed there, cross the bridge on the northern side of the town, return to the Danube and try the Bertholdsheim ferry and the Marxheim Bridge; we thought both of these would probably be guarded and, if so, we planned to follow the north bank of the Danube down to Donauworth.

We realised that at least thirty, and possibly over double that number had escaped, and that the Germans would probably take more trouble to recapture us than after the Warburg escape but never visualised what the calling out of the Landwache would entail. We learnt later that sixty thousand members of this force, armed with anything from pick-helves to punt-guns, were patrolling the local area and, in view of this, it seems a miracle that we survived as long as we did.

The night's march started well. After going straight across country for about a mile, partly through standing corn, we hit the road and carried on down it for some way, still glancing over our shoulders from time to time in case we were being followed. By 2300 hours it was almost pitch dark and the cloudy sky was continually obscuring the North Star. We entered some dense fir woods marked by their heavy oppressive atmosphere and very nearly ran into trouble. A match was struck by someone lighting his pipe just ahead. We easily avoided him by a short detour and emerged on the outskirts of Cietlhausen through which we passed to the inevitable accompaniment of barking dogs.

After this we took a wrong turning. My memory as to where or when is hazy but on the far side of the next village we found ourselves heading north. We took a rest and a drink in a cornfield and presently heard the dogs starting up again. We wondered whether this was Dougie Moir's party which we knew was taking the same route as ourselves. We returned into the village where we again became lost – this time heading due east. We finally left it behind heading in the right direction but we were nowhere near where we had hoped. The village sign-board showed we had just left Laisake, which our map marked a few miles west of Neuburg. Instead of going south-west, we must have been going south-east.

From then onwards I carried the compass in my hand checking our direction at every turning in order to avoid similar mistakes. The road gradually deteriorated, a gateway loomed ahead followed by another, the path merged into a series of cart-rucks and finally even these disappeared. We walked on across the fields until we reached the edge of an apparently impenetrable forest, tired, thirsty and encouraged by our own incompetence. We adopted our usual remedy – a rest, a drink and a lump of sugar; while we lay in the long grass contemplating the wood I wondered why, when one's water-bottle was empty and tongue hanging out, one always imagined the sound of running water. We summoned up our courage and plunged blindly into the wood and were soon struggling amid branches, brambles and every conceivable obstruction. We persevered for perhaps 300 yards and suddenly, after extricating ourselves from a rhododendron thicket, we emerged into the open and there, roaring past our feet, was the river Danube.

There was no mistaking the river. Although little if any broader than the Thames at Windsor its powerful current, strengthened by the

waters of the Leck which flowed in thirty miles upstream, gave one
a feeling of irresistible strength. We paused to admire it and wonder
at the hundreds of miles those waters had yet to flow, before emerging
into the Black Sea. We filled our water bottles and had a long drink
before setting off along the bank. The sides of the river fell sheer, and
in parts had crumbled away altogether. It would have been easy in
the darkness to take a false step and find oneself being washed rapidly
away, loaded down by a twenty-pound pack, so we rather self-
consciously tied ourselves together with some string and I led the
way. Periodically I would fall head-first into a ditch and Martin would
strike as if he had hooked a tunny. Then he would sympathetically
help me out and on we went. Once I trod on a shell and felt the
crackling crunch under my boot. Hoping to find a duck's nest we
stopped and explored the ground with our hands but eventually
discovered a squashed snail. It soon dawned on us that the current of
the river was far too swift to allow of any pleasure boating and it
seemed unlikely that we should find what we wanted. So when the
river bank became too rough for further progress, we left it and
decided to make for Steppberg.

We hit the tributary of the Danube at about 0230 hours and were
greeted by a chorus of frogs. It resembled more the hoarse quacking
of ducks than the 'brek-ek-ek-ex koax koax' which Aristophanes
heard and the noise was tremendous. After walking about a mile
along the stream we spotted the outline of a boat lying in some reeds.
We rushed forward eagerly but our spirits fell when we found it was
sunk deep in the mud and had practically no bottom. At about 0315
hours we arrived at the point where the stream runs into the Danube.
The confluence was overlooked by a very steep hill on top of which
stood a chapel. A long flight of steps led down on the far or northern
side into the village of Steppberg.

By now it was growing light and we started to look for a hide.
There were no woods for miles around. We investigated a thick
hedgerow and some corn stocks but decided that we should be too
confined in either. We then explored the chapel and, although it
appeared to be disused, we could not be certain. We made enough
noise in the shrubs all round to waken the dead.

We then turned to the bushes on the hillside overlooking the
stream but decided that the slope was so steep that we should get little

or no rest. Moreover we heard voices on the path below which made us decide quite definitely against that spot. It was lucky that they did not hear us for we later learnt that they were men of the Landwache who nearly caught Dougie's party as they were preparing to row downstream into the Danube.

We returned to the main river and found what appeared to be the best available place. It felt damp and uncomfortable in the low ground, and Martin with difficulty repressed his misgivings, but I felt that anything was better than the chance of being spotted wandering about at that hour of the morning. I slept well for a couple of hours and woke to find our hide looking much more promising. The sun soon dried out the branches and the ground and by clearing the sticks and stones we made ourselves more comfortable. We draped some leafy branches over the 'doorway' and hung up our wet socks on the bushes to catch the sunlight. It was a lovely day and, between eating and sleeping, we abandoned ourselves to the enjoyment of our freedom, our beautiful surroundings and the birds which were never silent. We were temporarily disturbed by a horse and cart passing within a few yards along a track we had never noticed but the undergrowth was so thick that we never had a moment's anxiety.

In the afternoon we discussed plans for crossing the Danube. We decided that, if we failed to find a boat, we must cross the tributary north of Rennertshofen and first try the ferry at Bertholdshein then the Marxheim and Donanworth bridges; we would keep to the river bank all the way. Meanwhile it seemed a golden opportunity, as we were within a few yards of the river and in very good cover, to reconnoitre the immediate area in daylight. We both had a hunch, amounting almost to a conviction, that there must be some means of crossing at Steppberg although our maps gave no such indication.

Martin decided to go alone. He left immediately after 'tea', looking a bit odd in his home-made Gebirgsjaeger cap, the Colonel's waistcoat and battle dress trousers. He was determined to be seen by no-one so there was little to worry about. He seemed to be away for hours, though actually it was little over seventy minutes, during which time I perused the map and learnt by heart the position of every landmark we might pass in the coming night's march. Then, as I was beginning to grow anxious as to whether he had run into somebody or lost his way back to the hide, I heard a crackle of twigs and there he was – 5 yards away. He was streaming with sweat and obviously taking pains to control his excitement.

He had found a boat only three hundred yards from where we lay. It was a ferry to take pedestrians across the river and back. The boat was about twenty-five feet long and attached to the bows was a wire hawser; the other end of this ran along an overhead line stretching across to the other bank to prevent it from being washed downstream by the current. From the side of the hill he had watched two people being ferried across by an old boatman who only used one oar – the upstream or starboard one – the boat being kept straight by a rudder and the hawser. The only drawbacks were that the hawser made a certain amount of noise running along the overhead line and the boat was padlocked to a block of concrete. However we reckoned on unhooking the hawser if necessary and half an hour's work with our knives should solve the problem of the padlock. The reassuring factor was that, as far as he could see, the boat was definitely not guarded and almost certainly spent the night on our bank.

Our spirits soared. The boat seemed to have been sent from heaven and nothing could now stop us crossing that night. We dined in great form and set about brewing the tea. Hardly had the smokeless heater got going than we heard footsteps, the crackle of dry twigs and voices. I turned the machine upside down, smothered it with my greatcoat and lay on top, hoping no smoke was escaping. Some soldiers came down the path peering into the bushes on either side. They looked straight at us but we were so well hidden that they noticed nothing and we thought we were safe. The fire had behaved well, going out immediately and practically no smoke had escaped.

We stayed where we were, dead still and in a few minutes heard the voices of the men returning. This time they left the path and parted the bushes of our hide. They saw us at once and a tremendous uproar ensued. Yells of 'aus, auf' and 'Hände hoch' were mingled with cries for help to the others. They arrived at the double and we were surrounded by three soldiers and a civilian. They allowed us to collect our kit and to leave anything we did not want behind and we were marched off to the village of Steppberg. On the way we passed the boat. It looked horribly enticing and the Germans gloated.

We were taken through the village to the Burgomaster's house, which served as the local pub. Beer was produced and a crowd quickly gathered round to inspect us – farm labourers, gawky youths in shorts, old men and women, a few land girls – pretty, vivacious and very friendly as soon as they realised we were not Russians. A man in civilian clothes who looked typical of all that we were fighting against strolled up to us. He turned out to be an officer on leave and was quite charming. An NCO who had returned from telephoning Neuburg with orders to search us started shouting and throwing his weight about but was quickly told off by the officer.

We repaired to the Burgomaster's kitchen to await the arrival of our escort. It was hot as an oven and, though spotlessly clean, was swarming with flies. An attractive land girl entertained us by showing off her ducklings, curling her hair with hot tongs and giving us a basin of hot water to wash in. We were not hungry, so we left our food in our haversacks, hoping for a further chance to escape.

At about 2200 hours an officer and six guards arrived to take us back to Neuburg. It was a pleasant walk of about seven miles and we arrived at midnight. We were locked in a civil goal where we spent the next day. I have vague memories of an obsequious door-keeper, who fancied that he understood the English 'jentleman' but lost his temper when I would not sign his book, and of various anaemic cripples who brought us our food and bedding. There was a ceaseless clanking of doors and jingle of keys. Our cells were furnished sparingly, with a large commode in the corner containing some evil–smelling disinfectant. Soon after lunch Martin and I both felt sick and we spent the afternoon making short rushes to the bucket. It was a great relief when we heard that a lorry had arrived to take us back to the camp. It had been doing a round tour of the neighbourhood picking up twos and threes from almost every village.

It was depressing to find that so many had already been recaptured. The back of the lorry was packed tight with people, but arriving back we found that only very few survivors were still out. We spent an uncomfortable night on the floor of some cells and the next day over fifty of us were crowded into a pink bus opposite the Commandantür. All our belongings, hastily collected and packed by our friends, were thrust onto us by the Germans and the squalor and congestion of that room became indescribable.

The following evening we were moved up to Willebaldburgs Schloss, a large white mediaeval castle standing high up on top of a hill about four miles away. It could be plainly seen from the camp. It was there that the Dieppe prisoners had been handcuffed. There followed as unpleasant a fortnight as I can ever remember. We were starved on dried turnip soup, at which my stomach quickly revolted, and I spent most of the time in bed with diarrhoea, thus missing much of the boredom. But conditions in the subterranean vault in which we lived were worse than anything I had hitherto experienced, and I shall never forget the open 'abort' with a hundred foot air shaft up which a strong draught blew – carrying with it the paper one had just dropped and an all-prevailing stench. Colonel Merritt VC, our senior officer, dealt with the whole situation magnificently and, thanks to his example, everyone remained in tolerably good form.

But it was a great moment when the uncertainty of our future came to an end and, on 21 June 1943, seventeen days after the night of our escape, I left with the first party by train for Oflag IVc.

[With hindsight our future was not at all secure. Orders were, in fact, being prepared which laid down the death penalty for all prisoners of war who were recaptured after an escape. These orders were finally promulgated after the attempt on Hitler's life in July 1944 and were first applied when some seventy-five officers escaped from a tunnel at Sagen. The ashes of some fifty of them were subsequently returned to the camp. Later I learnt that the German High Command had ordered our party to be segregated at Willebaldburgs Schloss pending a decision as to whether or not we should be the first victims of this new policy.]

Chapter 11

Colditz

The journey was uneventful. Each carriage was guarded by a sentry and no-one made an attempt to jump the train. This I think was due less to the German precautions than the feeling of weakness after a fortnight's starvation in the Willebaldburgs Schloss and that each minute took us further from a friendly frontier. We spent a hot and thirsty night in our little carriage, with Jack Fawous stretched out in the luggage rack, Martin, two others and myself on the floor or under the seat and, typically enough, Charlie Hopetoun pigging it on the seat; Charlie's quest for comfort was too ingenuous even for us to resent.

As we approached the little Saxon village of Colditz we crowded eagerly to the windows to see what our future prison looked like. The first impression was not encouraging – a gigantic schloss with barred windows. Standing upright on a sheer hillock and surrounded by many miles of wire and sentry boxes perched on top of tall poles, it looked depressing to live in and hard to escape from.

We were marched through the village in the gathering twilight. As we came to a bridge over the river Möhlde we came into full view of the castle and a mighty cheer rose from it. Every window had faces pressed against the bars – people who had been waiting there for hours to get a first view of the new arrivals and to give them a welcome. We felt heartened by this and we marched on with a lighter step speculating on whom we should find inside. It was a change to feel welcome at a new camp. Usually one was met by the long faces of selfish men who resented the arrival of newcomers because it meant more overcrowding and less of those precious elusive things called privileges.

The customary search before we were admitted into the camp was more thorough and intimate than any I had so far experienced. I had a small compass which I planned to hide in my mouth. But Charlie Hopetoun, who was searched before me, managed to signal before leaving the room by opening his mouth wide. So I coughed it into my hand and, as I took off my shoes, I laid it behind a bench and got away with it

As soon as we had been searched we were released into the camp. It was dark now and, as the great gates were opened, we walked into a courtyard entirely surrounded by buildings four storeys high. From every window people were shouting to us, trying to find out who we were and we, too, tried to identify their voices. The excitement caused by our arrival was unlike anything I had known before and made me realise what a big event in their lives this must be. Many, we know, had spent the whole war in this castle.

As we arrived at one of the four stairways leading up into the buildings, Martin and I were met by Gris and Mike Sinclair. It was over two years since I had last seen them, being carried out of Posen in a rubbish cart, hidden in a sack under piles of swill. Since that day they had spent nearly a year at large in Poland and many other occupied countries in Europe, and their adventures – especially those of Mike – could fill several volumes. We were overjoyed to meet again and experienced that feeling of having so much to say that one can say nothing. We were quite incoherent. They were wonderful to us, fixing up our sleeping quarters and giving us a delicious stew and brew after brew of cocoa which they had saved from their own parcels. It was an unforgettable evening and a foretaste, as we felt afterwards, of the joys we anticipated on meeting our families for the first time when we returned to England.

Next day we had time to look round and take stock of our new surroundings and companions. The castle was not unlike that at Tittmönning. But the courtyard was entirely surrounded by high buildings and this was to be our main exercise ground. Out there every morning would be seen bodies lying on rugs waving their feet in the air and doing stomach exercises and physical jerks. Later in the day a steady stream would circulate round the small yard with the glazed stare of men whose thoughts are dulled by monotony and their eyes starved of normal sights.

There was another exercise ground, it is true. The Germans called it the 'Park' and there we are allowed to exercise for an hour or two in the afternoon. But the compulsory formalities before reaching the Park were ludicrous and, after a time, exasperating. A queue would form at the appointed hour at the gates of the courtyard, and a German officer would count the people waiting. They were then allowed to pass through the gate into an alley lined with soldiers with rifles at the ready and would be counted again. Another gate would then be opened and, hemmed in by this line of 'guns' still at the ready, the queue of officers would be escorted down a path with barbed wire on either side into a paddock surrounded by two fences of wire six feet high. Here they would again be counted. At last, after the guards had taken up their positions, the German officer would give a gracious bow and a *'Bitte, Meine Herren'* as they would be allowed the privilege of rotating around this field which was perhaps double the size of the courtyard. These formalities, at first comic, became exasperating and few people had the self-control to bear it regularly. But the feel of turf under one's feet and the sight of trees drew one there, particularly in the spring when the birds were singing.

The castle buildings were old, but the living quarters allowed more space than we had hitherto experienced. Through the bars of the windows one looked out over the village of Colditz to the flat plains of Saxony which stretched for miles into the distance – good farming country broken up by large woods. It was a strange view. The castle was so high up that one had the feeling of looking out of an aeroplane over the roof tops of the village.

The great excitement of our first day was the discovery of our new companions. There were several old friends, besides Mike and Gris, who had been with us at one time or another, 'dirtied their copy-book' and ended up in what was known as the *'Straflager'*. [This term always brought a cry of protest from the Germans who would say indignantly 'This is not a *'Straflager'*, it is a *'Sonderlager'*. But the difference between a 'punishment camp' and a 'special camp' was lost to us.]

Douglas Bader was one of the first faces to appear next morning. I had last seen him at Warburg in the summer of 1942 when he was moved on to an Air Force camp. Since then he had got himself sent on to a troops camp by changing his identity with someone else and had escaped. He and his friends were all captured on an airfield where they had hoped to seize a plane; they identified him by ordering them all to take their trousers down. Peter Dollar had arrived here as a result of a bit of trouble in a 'Goon baiting' episode at Spangenburg. Goon was now the universal term for the Germans and was well suited to their character.

Colin Mackenzie was an old friend who had been at Eton with me. He was almost an original inhabitant of Colditz, having been sent there from Tittmönning where he had an unfortunate fiasco – being discovered in a rubbish cart by a child of six just as he had got out of the camp. Colin joined our mess, which was otherwise composed of Martin, Charlie Hopetoun, Charlie Weld-Forrester, Pat Campbell-Preston, David Walker, John Arundell and Jack Fawous. We soon became known as the Bullingdon which was a peculiarly apt nickname. Charlie Hopetoun was, I think, the only genuine member of this club but the others were mostly OEs with the necessary 'old-school' and horsey characteristics. This sounds a most unattractive collection of people but in fact we got on wonderfully well together and made friendships which will last a life-time. We had our rows and upheavals but our mess stood the test of time.

The camp included a most cosmopolitan collection. The majority were French. These were divided into two inimical parties – de Gaullists from North African, where most of them had been in the Special Forces and the pro-Petain Frenchmen who had been captured in 1940. The latter were devotedly loyal to the old Marshal for whom they had the greatest respect even if they sometimes disagreed with his policies. They received parcels from the Vichy government and were quite well looked after.

The de Gaullists, on the other hand, thoroughly despised anyone who could associate himself with the Vichy government. They wore battle-dress, lived with us and received British Red Cross parcels, and became in some cases more British than the British, threatening their compatriots with hanging after the war. The French numbered roughly a hundred. Next in numbers in the camp were some thirty Poles. Very smart and well-disciplined they could never quite forget that they were Polish officers entrusted with the protection of their national honour. They were alarming people, who had fought with fanatical courage, but one always had to be on one's guard against offending them.

Then there were a handful of Belgians and two Czechs. Of the latter Lieutenant Chalupka [Czecho] was one of the most attractive and colourful personalities in the camp. He had escaped from his country to England in 1938 when he was adopted by Eric Linklater and spent all his leave at the Linklaters' home. He was shot down during the Battle of Britain by one of our own pilots and so to Colditz. He was a huge black-haired chap with a wonderful physique of which he was very proud. Considering his age his reputation as a lady killer showed a very early development. He played all games with tremendous energy but, like all Central Europeans, he could not understand that British business about being a good loser. He was a great exhibitionist. But above all he was known and respected for his dealings with the Germans. There was not a soldier who joined the battalion guarding us whom Czecho did not know personally and contact on every possible occasion. As a black marketer he had no equal and the information which he extorted from them was of the greatest value. It was seldom that the Germans did anything affecting us, such as a search, without him getting a few hours warning and, if it was necessary for a sentry to be looking in a certain direction at a certain time, Czecho had to be contacted. He was a most ingenuous and generous character whom none of us will ever forget but sadly he was killed in an aeroplane crash shortly after the war.

There had been a lot of Dutch in the camp. But they had all left a few weeks ago. I was sorry and missed them as the British got on with them better than other foreigners – and as escapers they were by far the best.

My first impression of the camp was the astonishingly high morale which existed. It seemed strange at first that this should be so, as conditions were far more austere than in any camp I had previously known, and many of the officers had been there for three and a half years with no hope of moving on to a better one. But the reason lay partly in the very conditions and partly in the officers themselves. The fact that the *Straflager* received special treatment gave an air of distinction to the place. People came to talk of graduating to the *Straflager* and considered it an acknowledgement by the Germans of their escaping prowess or of their nuisance value.

And so it was the cream of officers of the allied prisoners of war who were collected there – people who had escaped once, twice or many more times, Dutchmen who preferred five years of captivity to signing away their honour to the Germans, mysterious men who had been picked up behind the enemy lines in North Africa, France, Albania or Yugoslavia. Every man in the camp had an interesting past and there were few of the 'passengers' who formed the vast majority of the other camps.

There was, however, in Colditz a minority who became known as the 'Men of Spirit'. For the most part their escaping record was not impressive but they were exhibitionists of the first order. And we were the audience for which they had long been waiting. They spent their time shouting insults at the 'Goons' from behind the protection of a convenient number of people and throwing paper-bags filled with water at German guards in the courtyard below. Although hooliganism was extremely effective when controlled and for a definite purpose the activities of the men of the spirit often caused unnecessary interruption of more important work and sometimes very real danger to life. One Frenchman was wounded through the shoulder while reading a book after a volley of shots was fired in retaliation for a water bomb.

The escaping record of Colditz's PoWs was indeed remarkable. Despite the fact that it had three separate lines of defence round the moat and that there were more guards than prisoners, escapes were not only frequent but highly successful. Their frequency was partly due to the feeling of competition between the different nationalities, which spurred incredible acts of courage and ingenuity. Their success was due to the information collected there by people of all nationalities who had escaped in every conceivable way and made their way by various means towards the frontier of their choice. Before escaping one was equipped with the normal necessities – civilian clothes, food, compass and maps. But here, in addition, one was provided with a sketch map of the exact position of the frontier to be crossed, showing sentry posts, their beats and the minutest details. Further, the forged papers were first class as I came to know after working in that department for several months. We also knew addresses of people who were prepared to lend assistance on the way to the frontiers and at the Baltic ports where ships left for Sweden.

At the time of my arrival a roll of honour of successfully escaped prisoners was kept hung up in Colditz. It included names of eight allied officers, including Ronnie Littledale, who had got to England with two Dutchmen a few months previously.

During our first day or two we became more and more convinced that we had arrived at a mad-house and we were the easy victims of one practical joke after another. We were told that there was a Russian General in the camp who wished to address the new arrivals and so we made a slight attempt to smarten ourselves up by standing fast when the remainder were dismissed from parade. A minute or two later a magnificent figure appeared in black overalls, a green jacket, red scarf, astrakhan hat and three inch moustaches. We sprang to attention and for five minutes were treated to a fluent speech, ably interpreted by Andy Anderson, in which the General expressed his pleasure at meeting us, his fighting brothers who, he was confident, would not relax until the last German in the camp was swinging from the lamp post, high above the courtyard. This speech was well received by us and Charlie Hopetoun replied suitably. Only later did some of us wonder why the Germans, who had been listening to this speech, were so amused at our looks of admiration at the speaker and his sentiments. The Russian General was a marine called Darby Rogers.

The same evening we had been told the Chinese Admiral wished to make our acquaintance and, being of a truly democratic nature, asked if he could take coffee with us after supper. We were naturally suspicious as by now most people realised that their legs had been pulled that morning. But we prepared to entertain him, produced a wooden chair with arms and a rather smaller mug than the rest, which might pass for a coffee-cup. The Admiral arrived and even the most suspicious of us had to admit that here was a genuine Chinaman in a very splendid naval uniform. He advanced with hands together, pointed forward like a Roman Catholic, bowed with a slight hiss and said 'No speaky Inglese.' After we'd all shaken hands, bowed and been blown a kiss, he spoke volubly in Chinese and, considering he had no interpreter, it was remarkable how long the conversation was kept up.

After about 20 minutes he rose gracefully, shook hands with a bow and blew another kiss to us all and it was not till he'd reached the door that a remark was heard from the corner of his mouth, which sounded to those nearby uncommonly like 'How d'yer legs feel?'

We realised we'd fallen a second time. In fact the Admiral was a Malayan in the Merchant Navy and a very popular figure in the camp.

Nettled by our own gullibility we were determined that the rear party, when they arrived from the schloss, should not get away with it. So we laid on a rather cruel ceremony. Soon after their arrival we started circulating stories of the eccentric German MO who would probably inspect them all to-morrow morning. While they were still in bed sleeping off the effects of their journey from Eichstätt, there was the noise of tramping boots, an angry German roar and in swept the MO followed by his orderly. All the new arrivals were ordered out of bed to line up for inspection and my services were called for as interpreter. I had to explain that, owing to the danger of typhus, strict precautions had to be taken to ensure nobody was lousy.

One by one the officers were brought up before the MO, stripped stark naked, treated to a fluent abuse in German and condemned to have the hairy parts of their body painted with an unpleasant sticky green mixture. John Arundell was the first to be called up and as he suffered this indignity, I could not help thinking of his eighteen generations of forbears, some of whom too had been persecuted and sent to prison, turning in their graves at this latest outrage. Some officers resented this treatment strongly and Edmund Hanney had to be put in close arrest. But the bluff was kept up and no-one suspected that it was Howard Gee, a civilian internee, who was painting their balls with a mixture of green paint and sticking paste. The party finally broke up in disorder when I stole the MO's stethoscope. [David Walker was heard half an hour later saying 'These bloody men of spirit, why they steal a useless stethoscope, God knows. Now we'll have another search'.]

The impression that we had arrived in a madhouse was brought home by the many eccentrics in the camp. Various factors were responsible for making people go 'odd', but the austere conditions and the fact that some officers had been there over three years were the main reasons. Eccentricity showed itself in very different forms. In its mildest, the individual would withdraw into himself, his eyebrows became permanently puckered and he would become morose. He would walk round the courtyard for hours on end alone with his thoughts shunning companionship. One officer, at least, got into this state by simulating lunacy in the hope of being repatriated and achieved the ambition two years later as a genuine case. Pretending to go mad in prison is, to my mind, the most dangerous thing a man can do. Anyone who has read *The Road to Endor* and heard the fate of the officers who escaped by this means will readily understand the danger. Living the unnatural life of a prisoner one must unconsciously keep one's self control on a tight rein. Any relaxation caused by simulated lunacy makes it hard and often impossible to regain that self-control. Considering the aggravating circumstances it is amazing how few people did go mad but there were more casualties than in any other camp I know and, in the last few weeks of the war, many were near breaking point. This would seem to contradict my description of the high morale but Colditz was a camp of extremes and I was referring to the large majority.

During the first two or three weeks the camp was in a state of flux with the departure of all the Dutch, Belgians, and the pro-Petain French. This exodus occurring soon after our arrival, afforded a very good opportunity of hoaxing the Germans. One of our team would exchange identities with a Frenchman who looked reasonably like him. If he got through the identity check successfully, having previously learnt by heart the necessary answers to questions such as 'mother's maiden name' etc., he would go with the French to their new camp. Usually the train afforded a chance to escape but, if that failed, the new camp was full of possibilities compared with Colditz. Once his true identity was discovered the officer would return to Colditz a few weeks later and his double would then be dispatched. This hoax worked time after time. The participant would have a trip across Germany with a good chance of escape in return for a couple of weeks' confinement in the cooler; it seemed a price well worth paying. Despite multiple efforts the Germans failed to devise any means of stopping the game.

One day, just after a large party of French had left, I saw a *Feldwebel* eyeing me suspiciously on parade. I got behind another officer to see whether it was really me he was after. He followed me round and next minute I found myself arrested between two guards. For a moment I was quite mystified but then the *Feldwebel* smiled truculently and said, 'You can't deceive us, you know, not even behind those dark glasses.'

I realised that they had mistaken me for one of the party of Frenchmen and Belgians who had left that day thinking I was masquerading as an Englishman. As I was taken off to the Commandant's Office I shot a remark at a Frenchman which further convinced the Germans. After an hour's grilling by the Security Officer we came to an impasse. I gave him my name and number correctly but got my family's names and addresses wrong. The Germans, convinced now that I was a Belgian, declared that they had no intention of treating as a PoW someone whose identity could not be proved. I declared that I had stated my name and number correctly and was required to give no more details. I was interviewed daily for a week in the hope of being sent off for a stay in the Belgian camp at Lübeck. As he feared making a further mistake the Security Officer gave up. 'We do not know who you are,' he said, 'but we know you are not Pardoe.'

The departure of the French, Dutch and Belgians was a blow to the camp, which thereafter lost much of its international character and individuality. They were stimulating companions. The French had a fine technique of dealing with the Germans. They taught us a lot and kept us alive. On their departure, the camp became more British – we missed the French cooks, we became 'organized' and we retired more into ourselves.

We soon became involved in the 'Parole' controversy. The Germans had originally offered parole walks to all nationalities except the Poles. Most people felt that this was an insult which should be fought. Those who accepted the bait were booed with cries of *'collaborateurs'*. So the park walks stopped. The Germans, keen to keep the door open, then offered walks to everybody with the exception of three specially guarded prisoners – Giles Romilly, Michael Alexander, and Charlie Hopetoun. Again we refused after much discussion and argument. Eventually the Germans, perhaps tongue in cheek, offered the walks to these very three officers on whose behalf we had refused and, to everyone's amazement, they accepted. Three days a week they gave their parole not to escape and, surrounded by more guards armed with machine guns and accompanied by dogs, this strange party would set off for an hour's tramp around the country.

The question of whether or not parole walks should be allowed is a difficult one, and the decision should always have been made by the senior officer of the Camp – not by individuals. Obviously it was in the interests of the Germans that they should be allowed. Their propaganda value with the outside world was great. They economised guards, they precluded escape, and the giving of parole for one thing was the thin end of the wedge for another. In view of this and the regulations governing the granting of parole it could seem hard to justify. On the other hand in an overcrowded small camp without adequate exercise facilities health and morale were bound to deteriorate. Given the conditions I felt that the acceptance was justified. In many camps, however, parole was given far too often in outrageous circumstances; we despised these as 'holiday camps'.

I do not criticise Charlie Hopetoun and the other *prominenti* for taking their walks. They were all being specially guarded for various reasons – Charlie for being his father's son, Giles Romilly because his mother was a sister of Mrs Winston Churchill. Michael Alexander had been caught in German uniform behind the lines and avoided a firing squad by declaring that General Alexander was his uncle – quite untrue. German guards had to report them present six times a day and they were locked up at night in special rooms. Their treatment can best be described as being 'persecuted with privileges'. This special attention caused them particular worry when, with the war nearing its end, it was known that they were being so guarded on Himmler's orders.

We were relieved to learn that Colditz was equipped with a wireless set which was taken over by the British when the French left. News services were delivered nightly and we soon heard of the Italian Armistice which had been so long expected. The Russian advance to Smolensk was also encouraging and we got much pleasure from watching the flow of events on our maps and marking in red chalk the vast areas liberated by the Russians.

I doubt if there was a camp in Germany without its wireless set and yet the Germans spent more time trying to find them than anything else. They knew we had the set but its location and how we obtained it was beyond them. There were three principal methods of acquiring a wireless set. The easiest was to bribe a foreign worker or a German to bring one into the camp. Another successful and relatively trouble-free technique was to have the valves sent out from England in tobacco tins and get some genius to construct the rest. The third method was to get some organization at home to send a complete wireless set out in a parcel which could be intercepted before the Germans opened it. Given warning of the arrival of the parcel this was not difficult.

The parcels would arrive one day and a British representative would make a list of them with the German NCO. If he saw an 'interesting' parcel the representative would warn the recipient to keep out of the way that day and not claim it. That night, after the parcels store had been locked and the burglar alarm set, a little play would be enacted. Czecho would come down into the courtyard and start talking to the German sentry. The sentry would then disappear for a minute or so into an alley. During that minute, two officers who had been lounging near the alley leading to the parcels store would disappear into it. The electric current would be shorted, the lock picked and the suspicious parcel would be replaced by a parcel of books and games. The door would then be relocked, the sentry diverted once more and the booty was ours. In this simple manner a wireless set, tool kit, maps, passes, money, etc., were secured, and automatically became controlled by the Escape Committee.

For several months just after our arrival at Colditz I worked under Peter Dollar in the parcels office. The routine work was the issue of food parcels and tins which never contained contraband as they were sent by the Red Cross. Clothes parcels too were immune. It was the odd games parcel for which we kept our eyes skinned and we had memorized names of those who were expecting 'phoney' parcels. Anything passing through the Germans' hands was doomed as they were extremely experienced searchers and had an X-ray machine. They found and confiscated a lot of stuff but most of the important parcels got through.

I took up this work in the parcels store because I had no inclination to start tunnelling from the camp and I had to have some occupation. Tunnels had been attempted time and again. They were usually started on the 1st and 2nd floor, one even on the 4th floor, and worked down a buttress to below the cellars and out under the wire but not one succeeded. The most nearly successful led into the main sewers and a party had found their way well outside the camp when one of the German police dogs 'pointed' at a manhole and a very bedraggled 'sewer rat' was dragged up. It was most unpleasant working in such conditions where every abrasion went septic and chances of success were so remote.

Soon after our arrival Mike Sinclair asked Martin and me to help him in a most daring and ambitious escape attempt. The plan was originally conceived when someone noticed a remarkable likeness between Mike and a *FeldWebel* who, owing to the length of his bushy white moustache, was known as Franz Joseph. On the night when Franz Joseph was guard commander, Mike, suitably dressed for the part, accompanied by two ordinary sentries Lance Pope and John Hyde-Thompson, was to get out of a window [the bars having previously been filed] and walk round between the Castle and the wire as if inspecting the sentries at their posts.

On arrival at a certain spot Franz Joseph [Mike] would notice that the bars of another window had been filed away. Turning on the nearest genuine German sentry he would berate him, put him under the arrest of Lance Pope, while John Hyde-Thompson took his place. As soon as Lance had marched him off fifteen officers would slide down a blanket rope and away on John's beat.

My part was to signal the position of the sentries to Mike. The operation started well. Mike, Lance, and John got out of the window without being seen and, as they came into sight, they looked for all-the-world like three Germans. Mike stopped opposite the window, turned on the sentry and treated him to as voluble a flow of abuse as ever I've heard. The sentry was at first taken in completely, but when ordered to leave his post, he hesitated for about half a minute. In that half minute another NCO appeared. He had just been with the real Franz Joseph and saw through Mike at once. A shouting match between the two followed, the German's voice rising shrill as he yelled *'Hande Hoch, Hande Hoch.'* Mike stood his ground. Next minute there was the flash of a revolver and Mike slumped to the ground.

Consternation followed inside the camp as fifteen officers in civilian clothes tried to get back to their rooms and hide their escape kit before the Germans arrived. We were all called out on parade and waited anxiously for news of Mike who had been very lucky. The bullet had gone into his chest just below his heart and out at the side without touching a bone. Within a fortnight he was up and within three weeks he was preparing for another escape.

For me, time went fairly quickly as I kept myself busy. Most mornings I spent down in the parcels office. In the afternoons we would go down to 'the Park' or sunbathe in the courtyard. It was a horrible scene of semi-nuked bodies lying on the cobbled floor of this sun trap, but a pleasant way of attaining oblivion and physical satisfaction.

The courtyard was the scene of simultaneous activities; at the time of our arrival it was not uncommon to see a game of volley ball going on in the centre, while Douglas Bader and Andy knocked a tennis ball backwards and forward one end; others might be hurling a medicine ball at each other the other end, and individuals could be doing PT in various corners perhaps with John Arundell running round tor the 35th time – all this in addition to the normal crowd walking or coffee housing and enclosed within a space of about sixty yards by thirty.

The local game, the speciality of Colditz, was stoolball – a most admirable form of exercise. There were three forwards, one half, two backs and a 'stool keeper'. The object of the game was to touch the stool with the ball and there were virtually no rules. The game usually resolved itself in bitter turmoil round one stool or the other, with perhaps three forwards charging hard down at the stool behind which were walls of granite. Why no-one was killed I have no idea. People were hurled through the air and landed on the cobbles or against the walls with no apparent ill effects. It was also a great game for the spectators who, headed by Douglas Bader, yelled themselves hoarse. I must confess that, before each game, I felt like the gladiators of ancient Rome proclaiming '*morituri te salutamus*'; I had never so completely lost myself in the enjoyment of a game before.

The camp was equipped with a very beautiful Chapel bordering the courtyard. As successive tunnels were discovered under the altar or through the organ it was not surprising that it should always have been shut. A theatre too was also kept shut as a reprisal for some act of indiscipline and its reopening was always held out as an inducement to better behaviour.

My memory of Christmas 1943 is obscured by a haze of alcohol. Despite the fact that the Germans provided none we all managed to either acquire or make for ourselves some Schnapps with an alcoholic content of about 80 per cent. The making of it was a great art in which I became engrossed. Sugar, raisins and any fruit that could be acquired was put in the right quantities in jars of water and kept at a warm temperature next to the stove. Some yeast would start the fermentation and in a fortnight's time it would be ready for distilling. This was done by heating it to a temperature of about 80° and passing the alcoholic vapours through a rubber tube immersed in cold running water – out then poured the raw alcohol. It was then treated with burnt sugar to add taste and colour and there was as much brandy as we'd been praying for.

One orgy followed another. On Christmas Day itself we had a great dinner party followed by a midnight show put on by the orderlies in the courtyard. It was a fine sight with the walls and cobbles covered in snow. From different corners of the yard, preceded by the blaring of trumpets, a feudal lord and his supporters appeared in fancy dress with the lord mounted on something meant to resemble a horse. After the rivals had drawn up opposite each other and taken stock of their adversary there was another blare of trumpets and battle was joined. There were many sore heads next day. A fancy dress party the following night was enlivened by an amazing variety of clothes discarded by our departed foreign friends – and still the drink held out.

Early in the New Year I twice did a spell of ten days in the cells for deliberate minor offences committed in order to break the monotony of life. There were times when everybody including Martin, Pal and my best friends irritated me unbearably and I felt I must somehow get away from it all. The solitude of the cells was a healthy challenge. The first time I was put in the camp cells with Charlie Forrester and on the second I was sent down the town to the overflow cells. This made a complete change and was worth it if only for the glimpse of life as we were marched through the town.

In Colditz we were completely starved of normal sights and of colour. One could look out of the windows at the fields but always the view was marred by the window bars. In the courtyard one's eyes met grey walls and stone cobbles. I became short-sighted and my eyes felt strained and my eye-sight blurred when I looked at distant objects and worried about the permanent effect that this would have.

During the winter I joined the forging section. Every day for eight hours we worked in a room on the top floor of the Castle, guarded by our own 'stooges'. It was exacting work. For two months I practised eight hours a day before at last my boss 'Boggy' Beat passed my work as good enough. He had learnt under a brilliant Pole who must have been an expert before the war. There were always many men contemplating an escape so we were kept pretty busy. A good pass took anything up to fifteen hours to complete. The finished articles were most impressive and several successes were scored with them.

I gave up this work when I started working on my own plans to escape. I was prepared to consider any method other than tunnelling and the first idea came from Teddy Barton. Before the war Teddy had been a dress designer; in Colditz he became the principal 'stage director'. He was an expert make-up artist and one day it had dawned on him that I bore an astonishingly close resemblance to the camp commandant – Oberst Leutnant Prawitt. This man was an arrogant iron-disciplined Prussian with whom I can think of nothing I had in common and, to my disgust, I now recognised our physical similarity.

The plan was for me to walk out of the gate in his uniform after dark together with his usual attendants. I studied the plan carefully, watched Prawitt come in and go out of the camp three or four times a day for several weeks. But the sentries still scrutinised his pass and I came to the conclusion that the chances of success were too small to warrant the work put into making the uniform, maps, passes, etc. when we would almost certainly all be taken straight into the cells.

Then I thought of another plan. Our own quarters which were surrounded by many strands of wire, sentries and searchlights were at one place joined to the German quarters; these were surrounded only by a moat in which a sentry had a 350 yard beat. Once into the German quarters escape would be easy. This had long been realised but many attempts had been foiled; the Germans had wired the wall and any tampering was immediately given away by a burglar alarm. My plan was to get through the ceiling and work my way into the German quarters between the floor boards.

At the time I put up my plan to the committee two other parties had just put up a similar plan. One party was headed by Frank Weldon [later an Olympic equestrian gold medallist] and Hamilton-Baillie, the two engineers who were entirely responsible for the success of the Eichst□tt tunnel. The other party was Hector Christie and Lawrence Pope; both had been sent to Colditz after escaping from Eichst□tt disguised as a German General doing a tour of inspection of the camp.

It was agreed that we should join forces and seven of us started work immediately. Things went well from the beginning. An invisible trap was cut in the ceiling which was reached from a ladder which normally looked like ordinary duckboards in the wash house. No wires were found in the roof and to our surprise there was no necessity to work under the floor boards as there was a passage just under the eaves leading into the German wing.

Three different trap doors had to be carefully made in the walls which separated us from our objective. A huge padlock on an iron door had to be picked. But in a matter of weeks all obstacles had been overcome and Frank and H-B, who were in charge of operations, had reached the very room in which we could bend the bars and let ourselves down by a rope into the moat below.

Hector and I were going together, dressed in civilian clothes, with passes stating that we were Lithuanians returning from temporary duty in IG Farben Industries in Leipzig to our group in Prague. Our plan was to walk eighty miles across country to Prague where Czecho gave us the address of an agent. He would fit us out with our clothes and genuine passes which would get us up to the Baltic port of Danzig [Gdansk] with no trouble. There we had the address of some Poles who organised an underground service for escaped prisoners into Sweden. And so to home. It all seemed gloriously easy. The walk to Prague was no problem and our maps of the frontier were first class. We completed our preparations, gave our suits their final pressing, packed our food, maps, papers, compass. In two days' time we should be free again. The only regret I had was that Martin was not coming with me. But numbers on this plan had to be kept to a minimum. Hector was a very resourceful old friend and, after Martin, I couldn't have wished for a better partner.

The night of our escape had been carefully chosen. There was no moon and it followed a German holiday. This was necessary because the room in which the bars had to be bent was used by a German carpenter and it was essential to ensure against his arrival in the middle of the operation.

While Frank and H-B were bending the bars, my job was to watch for any German approaching the carpenter's room. This I could see from Peter Dollar's room in the '*Zaalhouse*' which was exactly opposite. I had been watching Germans coming and going for about twenty minutes when I caught sight of the wooden-legged carpenter coming across the moat, entering the camp and making for his shop. I signalled by opening the window and watched spellbound. In his best 'holiday' suit this diabolical looking old cripple went straight to the door. He stood there for a minute spellbound, then turned and yelled hysterically for help. Germans ran from every direction. Frank and H-B were caught red-handed. They made no attempt to escape, hoping that their route would not be discovered, but the Germans only took a few hours to find all four trap doors and our hopes were shattered.

Blinding, numbing depression descended on me. Never before had I been so confident of success. Previously [on the train at Donauwörth, before the wire at Warburg, and in the tunnels at Eichstätt] I had felt the chances of success were little more than fifty per cent while the danger was considerable. But this was a practically fool-proof method with virtually no chance of discovery. My final ambition to get home from the *Straflager* must be abandoned. Two days later it became known that, after escaping from a nearby camp, fifty RAF officers had been murdered by the Gestapo.

The story of this murder is now widely known and was frequently reported at the Nuremburg trials. As I heard from a survivor seventy-five officers escaped from the tunnel – most of them in civilian clothes with Czech papers heading for Prague. About twenty-five were caught in the next day or two by the Wehrmacht who returned them to the camp. The remaining fifty who were caught by the Gestapo, SS, SA, and local police were taken handcuffed to Torgau. After three weeks being starved there they were they were given a shovel and made to dig their own graves. Then, kneeling down in a row, they each received the 'Nickschuss' – a bullet through the back of the head. Their ashes were returned to the camp and Hector and I undoubtedly owe our lives to the wooden-legged German carpenter.

The reason for this mass murder has never been cleared up and perhaps never will be. It was a precedent, but was repeated several times in the months to come when, among others, Hugh Mackenzie was murdered. The German excuse was that the victims resisted arrest. My theory is that Himmler, who was in charge of the secret police, had reports of a highly organised attempt on Hitler's life to coincide with an uprising throughout Germany by all foreign workers and anti-Nazis. This materialised in the events of 20 July 1944, after which Graf Stauffenberg, General Witzleben and many thousands of other 'undesirables' were liquidated. As a prelude to this attempt I believe that Himmler expected mass escapes by key prisoners who would help organise the revolution and, to forestall this, he ordered that anyone found with forged papers should be shot without trial.

The news put an effective damper on our activities and Colonel Tod, the SBO, forbade any further escapes for the time being. Tod was the most remarkable senior officer I met in Germany. He had a distinguished record in both world wars, a magnificent appearance and a great personality with which he changed the camp from an undisciplined rabble of individualists into a highly disciplined and organised community. He held the respect of all nationalities and, with a British brigadier, four French and two Polish Generals he carried out the difficult task of command with the complete confidence of all nationalities and ranks.

One day in June, soon after the news of the capture of Rome, we were returning from a typical walk in the 'Park' and as soon as we entered the courtyard we sensed a certain atmosphere. People stood about in groups talking excitedly. Miles Reid – one of those people who are always 'au fait' with the most modern world affairs – advanced on Martin and me with a suppressed twinkle in his eye. 'It's true, at last,' he said, 'yes, and the Germans have admitted it. They've landed.' 'Where?' 'Why in Normandy of course. I always said it would be Normandy. The Germans claim to be pushing them back into the sea, but that's nothing to worry about. This is the big thing and the end is in sight now.'

No-one who was not in an occupied country could have had any idea what the invasion meant to us. It was the key that would open the first door of our prison. It was the prize which we had been discussing, arguing about and awaiting for years. It seems absurd but many people expected it in 1942. In 1943 it was confidently predicted before the testimonies of the Dieppe prisoners shattered our hopes. So 1944 it had to be but where and when had constantly preoccupied us throughout the year.

So here it was at last. That night we listened, word by word, to the broadcast describing it. The experience was unforgettable as our bodies tingled, our heads grew light, the reality of the other life took shape and liberty appeared as a possibility in the not so distant future. The march of events in France coloured our lives that spring and summer. Our hopes rose with the attempt on Hitler's life and the race through France; the Arnhem setback, before which our confidence were at its height, sobered us up and told us to prepare for yet one more Christmas in the bag.

Escape was no longer considered and we threw our energies into sport. A big volley ball competition was staged in the form of a handicap knock-out competition. Day after day crowds would line the courtyard, lay wagers of hundreds of pounds with the bookies, and howl themselves hoarse with enthusiasm. The Bullingdon team consisting of two Charlies [Hopetoun and Forrester], Pat Campbell-Preston and myself started shakily, but managed to get through one round after another by the narrowest of margins. We had great confidence in ourselves and backed ourselves to win each time, and, as nobody else ever expected it, we usually got a fair price. Our crowning triumph was beating the favourites in the semi-final, but we succumbed gloriously [and with very raw feet] to the grossly under-handicapped doctors team in the final.

That summer also brought great advances on the Eastern front. The Russians reached Warsaw and we followed closely the gallant rising of the Polish underground army under General Bor Komorovsky. After their final defeat Bor, together with a few of his staff, arrived at Colditz. He was a small alert little man with a dignified air and a very cruel mouth. We invited him to meals with our mess and soon became firm friends, conversing chiefly in French. From our talks and from a series of lectures he gave we heard at first hand the horrors of those two months which he has described in his book, *The Unconquerables*.

The Germans treated the Poles as *prominenti*. That is to say, they kept them in special accommodation and under special guard. But they did all they could for them in the hope of befriending them; in their stupid minds they believed that, as the Russians had let down General Bor, he would change sides. A Foreign Office official actually paid Bor a visit a week before the end of the war and put the case to him quite bluntly. 'My car is outside the gate', he said, 'a villa is waiting for you and your staff. You have only to say the word and you are free men, free to join with us in the underground war against Russia.' I asked him what he replied. 'I told him that Poland had the honour to be the first country at war with Germany. I could see no reason for changing that state of affairs.' Bor was a very loyal ally. I never heard him say a word against the Russians. Only in the facts which he described could one see the depths of the Russian betrayal of Poland. Not content with betraying him the Russians had declared Bor a war criminal and he was indeed fortunate not to have eventually been 'liberated' by them.

We had some other interesting newcomers. They arrived in small parties and always had a story of adventure to which we listened eagerly. Colonel Rasch was one of the earlier arrivals from Sicily who brought us red hot news of the landing. He was sent to Colditz because he was carrying a newspaper article describing how he had escaped from the Germans once before. David Stirling and Jack Pringle were two great assets to the camp. They were suspected, rightly, of organising a mass escape from Brunswick. The Germans got wind of if it and had moved the camp just too soon. David's reputation had preceded him. He started the war as a subaltern in the commandos and, while recovering from a parachute drop in hospital, the idea had dawned on him of forming the SAS. By personal drive and enlisting the support of Churchill and Wavell his project was approved; since then his adventures had become a by-word in Africa, England and Germany. The books written about him give little idea of his personality.

I quickly fell under his spell. It was impossible to get him to talk about himself but he gave the impression of a will-power against which it was impossible to stand. One day, as we were walking round the courtyard, he started talking of his plans when we were released. He said he would form a parachute brigade, half English and half American, which he would train in India and fly into China, whence they would split up and start organising resistance and sabotage on the long Japanese lines of communication to Malaya. It was his old African game on a far vaster scale.

When he had described it he said as an afterthought, 'Would you like to come too?' I had no hesitation. He planned to have one battalion officered entirely by ex-prisoners of war of his own choosing with the intention of having the pick of the bunch and showing the world that the prisoners of war were as good or better as the rest. Tom Stallard, the controller of the Warburg wire escape, was to be in command with Tony Rolt, Frank Weldon and David Walker as his squadron leaders; Martin [despite a gammy knee] and Grismond also planned to join. The thoughts and plans for this expedition coloured the last few months of my captivity and completely motivated me between my release and the Japanese surrender.

Another arrival in the camp that summer was a merchant seaman called Purdy. One or two people in the camp remembered having seen him before but could not remember much about him. Like all other new arrivals, he was interviewed by Colonel Young, our security officer, who, though not absolutely satisfied by his story, let him proceed into the camp. Later in the day, as a result of what some people told him, Young interviewed Purdy again and decided that his story was false. He was put under close arrest and I was the first sentry.

The position was highly embarrassing to both of us. He asked me if I had any writing paper as he wanted to write to his girlfriend in Berlin. I gave him a couple of sheets of paper but of course had no envelopes as we were only given letter cards. He finished his letter, folded the other sheet expertly into the form of an envelope, and asked me to get it posted. I later passed it to Colonel Young.

He appeared very highly strung and distressed at being arrested and at last could bear it no longer. 'It's no good,' he said, 'I must get it off my chest.' I told him that he must not expect me to treat what he said as confidential but he did not care.

'I was a bloody fool,' he said. 'I escaped from my camp last year and, knowing the address of a girl in Berlin, I thought I'd try and contact her, in the hope of getting papers and clothes. I found her eventually living in a bombed out basement. She was very unhappy and badly off and, well, you know what it is when you haven't seen a girl for a few years. We decided to stay on together for a bit. All went well for a few weeks until a stranger arrived one day. He said he knew I was an Englishman and that the police knew all about me. He said this could be dangerous for me and the girl. I quite saw his point. He then said my one way of saving her life would be by doing a little work for the Germans. The idea of this was horrible to me but, when I heard that it was only broadcasting and when I thought of that girl's life, well, what could I do?

'That was the beginning of my association with Joyce. They were a decent couple. Mrs Joyce was particularly nice to me. While I was working with them, I made friends with a man called Boyd-Carpenter, who had got into trouble in much the same way as myself. Together we decided to try and escape. We made our plans, collected our food and papers. Everything was just about ready, when one night I got a telephone call. "Come round to my flat right away." It was Boyd-Carpenter's voice, sounding very tense over the line.

'I wasted no time. When I got to the flat I found the door open. I thought he must have left and shouted upstairs. There was no answer. I went up into his study and there, on the floor, lay the body of my friend, murdered in cold blood. God knows how he knew they were after him. I don't. I panicked absolutely. I ran down those stairs out into the street with one thought only in my head. I've got to get out of Berlin. As I reached the door of our basement I slowed-up and tried to calm myself. Inside, waiting for me, was the stranger who had been round before. With him was an elderly Hauptman. *"Guten Abend,"* they said smiling. I looked around and saw my girl shivering and white with fright. But of course she didn't know about Boyd-Carpenter yet.

'"So now you know," they said, "what happens to people who try to trick us. But he was unlucky, of course. He had no girlfriend. If he had we wouldn't have hurt him." And they glanced at my girl on the sofa. "You have one chance of saving her from a horrible fate," they said. "Tomorrow Hauptman Eggers leaves Berlin for Colditz. There are a number of things going on in that camp, which he wishes to find out." What could I do? What would you have done?'

As he stopped talking I shook myself and felt as if I'd just woken from a dream of finishing reading a novel. My two hours guarding him were up – I was relieved. That night Purdy pretended to be asleep, slipped away from his guard out into the courtyard and was let straight into the German quarters.

Next day the Germans came into the camp with a crow bar and pickaxe, knocked a hole in one of the buttresses and disclosed a tunnel which had survived several searches in the past six months. They then went up to a cupboard on the second floor, knocked a hole in its false bottom and pulled out a reserve wireless set and a complete tool kit. Purdy had not wasted his few hours of freedom in the camp.

He spent several weeks in the German Commandantür before being taken away. I was told at the War Office after the war that he had been caught wearing the uniform of the German SS in Northern Italy but it was decided not to charge him for betraying the whereabouts of the tunnel and wireless set as it would have been too difficult to prove. Anyway he had more serious charges to face; I read the account of his trial with some interest. He was found not guilty of giving away intelligence to the Germans at Colditz, but guilty of joining the enemy forces for which I had believed he was shot but, in her book *The Meaning of Treason*, Rebecca West states that he was given a life sentence. He was a weak man who, once he had allowed the Germans to get a hold of him, went faster and faster down the road to ruin.

People continued to arrive in small parties that summer. A curious figure called Dick Jones caused a certain amount of interest. His father was Egyptian and his mother Italian. He had no nationality but had been educated in England and spoke seven dialects of Arabic and five European languages fluently. He had worked as an agent for us in the Abyssinian War in 1935 and, in this war too, he was caught behind the lines in Tunis doing similar work.

I asked him one day if he would go back to England after the war. 'Not straight away,' he said, 'because I've got to fetch my money from North Africa.' 'Can't you get your money cabled through?' I said. 'It's not as easy as that,' he replied. 'You see all my wealth is contained in a precious stone which I have buried in the desert. When the war ends I shall return to the desert and find my stone.'

Four spies arrived soon after from France. They too were of mixed nationality. Their leader Pierre de Vomecourt was a pure Frenchman and a baron of the *ancien régime*. Tony du Puis was French too. He was very popular with the British with a passion for all sport, but particularly hunting. Georges Abbot was a Greek by birth and Bill Reading an Englishman. They all spoke perfect French and had landed in France in 1941; working in the *Deuxième* bureau they had started organising the Maquis. They were arrested in 1942 and, by all normal laws of probability, should have been shot but Pierre de Vomecourt, a brilliant lawyer, made a wonderful bid for their lives. He was talking to the German officer who had arrested them and pointed at the lack of justice in Germany. The German Hauptman contested this strongly and the argument became very heated. Finally Pierre declared, 'We are French officers.' 'What if you are?' said the Hauptman, 'Then we should be treated like prisoners of war,' he declared. 'You will be treated like prisoners of war,' asserted the Hauptman.

At his trial Pierre de Vomecourt quoted this conversation and said that history would judge the justice of Germany on whether or not the word of this Hauptman was upheld. The Hauptman was called as a witness and confirmed his words. They were released from Fresnes and arrived at Colditz. Few people can have had such a remarkable escape from the hands of German law. Their stories of the six months in Fresnes described all the horrors that have since been broadcast to the world. To us, hearing of them from first hand, it seemed a miracle that they remained sane. Bill Reading's hair had indeed changed from black to snow white but their minds, especially that of Pierre, were as alive as ever and Pierre's name will certainly be heard of again in French politics – perhaps in conjunction with that of Clemenceau, a firm friend of his whom he admired greatly.

People arrived from Yugoslavia – one, an Englishman, who had jumped off a train on his way into Germany from Greece and served for several months under Mihailovic with the Chetniks. The other was a Russian who had been serving under Tito. They both had very different stories to tell, which all helped to fill our picture of life throughout occupied Europe – a picture which was perhaps fuller and better than available to anyone in England or in the fighting forces.

Three Americans arrived. They had been sent over to conclude an armistice with Hungary. The plan was for them to be dropped in a field near Budapest where they would be visited by a Hungarian minister who would fix up the details of the armistice with them. The plan miscarried when the Germans, in a *coup d'état* a few days later, took over full control of the country. And so they came to Colditz. Their chief, Colonel Florimund Duke, was a most delightful and clever man. He had been chief advertising agent of *Life* before the war and quickly became a popular figure with us all.

Four French Generals arrived shortly after. They had been in the castle from which General Giraud escaped. It was for the part they had played in helping him that they were sent to Colditz. The Germans had deceitfully tried to discredit Giraud by saying he had broken his parole. He was, in fact, let down on a rope from the third storey of a castle and had to crawl for a considerable distance between two sentry posts and cut through two wire fences; once outside a waiting car had collected him and within a very few days he was in North Africa.

The four generals were much worried about the fate of one of their companions who was to have come with them; at the last minute the Germans had said he would be coming on the next train. Ten days later they announced that he had been shot trying to escape. He was 70 and very nearly blind.

There was something unique about every prisoner at Colditz but Charlie Upham was one who merits a special mention. He was a very quiet modest little New Zealander who had spent his life sheep farming. During the war he was awarded the VC and bar. I would have loved to hear his story but one might as well have tried to squeeze water from a stone.

Three most unfortunate and tragic incidents occurred that autumn which caused us acute depression at the time. The subject of the first one was Edmund Hannay. I had known him ever since Tittmönning and always thought of him as a bit odd – perhaps as a result of six months solitary confinement in France in 1940. He was an ardent escaper and a devoted admirer of Hamilton-Baillie. He had escaped from the Eichstätt tunnel and had been working on our attempt through the roof in Colditz. From the day the planned escape was discovered Edmund's behaviour became stranger. At first he became obsessed in a study of the Pyramids. Then he concentrated on the Bible and became convinced that he had discovered its key; every sentence he read bore a new meaning for him which he would try to explain to his friends.

He would succumb to fits of crying and blubber as if in a state of melancholic intoxication. Finally he dressed himself up in his service dress and Sam Browne belt [normally he was the scruffiest dresser] and walked round the camp with a poker and a soup ladle in one hand and his Bible in the other. Things were now getting past a joke and becoming dangerous. The doctors tried to persuade the Germans to have him taken away but they were convinced that he was faking. The German doctor came into the camp one day and Edmund rushed up [with Bible, ladle, and poker] embracing him on both cheeks in the middle of the courtyard and knocked his hat off in the process. Still the Germans smiled knowingly as if it was a hoax.

Next day, as he was racing round in his now usual get-up, Edmund saw a cat running across the square. There was a roar from Edmund 'Halt! I adjure thee in the name of The Lord God of Hosts to stop!' And the cat stopped. Things now rapidly worsened with a consequent deterioration in the nerves of everyone in the camp. Day and night the prison would echo with his roars and howls and by day we would not walk about without risk of being embraced. The effect on those living near Edmund was becoming almost unbearable and their nerves were strained to breaking point. The Germans at last agreed to put him in the cells. They said that it would be impossible to move him and a British doctor gallantly volunteered to sleep next door. That night the howls were worse than ever but what we didn't know was that he was going completely hay-wire. The whole floor was torn up and the bars, which normally two men could only bend with a crow bar, were twisted by his enormous strength. Next day he left for an asylum and was repatriated. When I saw him later in England he was much recovered but he will be a wrecked man for life.

This was a shattering experience for us all. Lunacy is infectious and we were living so closely on top of each other that we all felt its effect. Nobody in Colditz could have felt confident of remaining sane. It was the terrible danger of which we were all aware and, to guard against it, we built up a habit of self-control without which we knew we would follow Edmund Hannay.

The next tragedy occurred soon after. The first I knew of it was when I was cooking just before tea time and heard a burst of rifle fire from the direction of the 'Park'. Everyone crowded to the window but little could be seen. We soon learnt that Mike Sinclair had been killed in his last bid for freedom. A ban on escaping still existed in the camp as a result of the R.A.F. murders. Mike had told no-one of his intention and had made no apparent preparations. He had been deeply moved by the news received a week before of the death of his former escaping partner, Ronnie Littledale, on the western front near Calais. He had been in tolerably good form and actually spent his last morning translating an official document into German for the SBO. On his way down to the 'Park' he told Tom Stallard how grateful he was to him for all the help he had given him in his escapes. Tom thought at the time that Mike must have finally abandoned all hopes of getting another chance.

Mike walked around the 'Park' entirely alone; suddenly he stepped over the trip wire and calmly begun to climb the wire exactly in front of the light machine gun post. The sentries on either side were not 50 yards away and ran towards him shouting at him to stop. Others shouted at him too. Lawrence Pope with great presence of mind yelled at the sentries in German, 'Do not shoot. Do not shoot. Can't you see he is mad?'

Mike dropped to the ground on the far side, staggered and then, with his face set in grim determination and defiance, started jogging slowly through the trees. Sentries fired their revolvers and he staggered once as if hit but carried on. After he had miraculously covered 100 yards a sentry from the far side of the 'Park', 200 yards away, fired through the trees and Mike fell. The bullet had hit him in the elbow and ricocheted into his heart.

So died the bravest man I have ever met and one of my best friends. His reasons for this supreme act of courage are known to perhaps ten people, certainly not more. The general opinion is that his mind was affected and that he chose a gallant form of suicide. I know that this was not so but his story must remain, for the time being, untold. His family are proud of the memory of a very wonderful son. His escaping record was far and away the most outstanding in Germany. His first escape was from Poland in 1940 when he remained at large for several months, crossed numerous frontiers and was eventually caught in Sofia. After a period in the hands of the Gestapo he made seven more attempts. On three of these he reached the frontiers of Holland, France and Switzerland. He was never happy unless preparing to escape. His preparations were ruthlessly efficient and thorough. He set himself the goal of escape and preferred to risk death rather than failure.

The third tragedy was John Arundell. I have hardly mentioned him although he was one of my best friends and in our mess for about three years. He was a unique character from a different century and almost a different world. He was the last of a long line of Arundells of Wardour. He had fine looking Roman features and very upright carriage and the most perfect manners I have ever met and never forgot them whatever circumstances in which he found himself. He was a brilliant and stimulating conversationalist and was exceptionally well read. His knowledge of art was very wide and I never found a subject on which he could not discourse. He was a Roman Catholic and, if he had lived in an earlier age, he would undoubtedly have joined an ascetic Order. Asceticism was the tragedy of his life. Every Lent he gave up smoking and subjected his body to the most violent physical exertions. The one vice he allowed himself was drink and there never was a more pleasant and amusing companion in his cups. He never lost self-control despite a vast capacity for alcohol.

During the Lent of 1944 John set about subjecting his body to more violent exertions than usual and would go to bed at night dripping with perspiration. Yet he would sleep on top of his flea-bag with one thin blanket over himself while most of us were shivering under four. It was a triumph of mind over matter. Every morning he would run round and round the courtyard. He got the most terrible chilblains, a pale flush came into his cheeks and he gradually lost weight. It was clear that he had consumption and was finally persuaded to go into hospital. But even there he escaped to have a cold shower on the coldest morning. He was transferred to a local sanatorium from which he wrote letters to us. I wish I had not lost the letter he wrote to me a week before he was repatriated. It was full of his usual conversation mixed with classical quotations and of course his health. Within two days of arriving home he died.

John was not the only one to be repatriated; Jack Fawous, the jockey, who had been in our mess all the time and was one of the kindest chaps I've ever known, also got home with a very bad skin disease. There was a number of Frenchmen with us too who had been passed by the repatriation board but the Germans refused at first to allow them to go. As a protest, when the British officers due to be repatriated were called not one of them would go. An armed guard was sent for who immediately became surrounded by a mob of us. The paradoxical situation occurred of an armed guard fighting their way through a crowd of prisoners in search of a few well-hidden British officers who refused to be repatriated without their French allies. The demonstration was a complete success. Rather than try to explain why the British representatives were not forthcoming the Germans allowed the French to go.

That winter was the worst, I think, of the whole war. It was bitterly cold. The allies were held up on the Siegfried Line and, even worse, Rundstedt's counter offensive through the Ardennes showed that the Germans still had some kick in them. We did not know the strength of the German defences and wondered whether the stalemate of the First World War had not once more set in. Flying bombs were smashing up London with depressing regularity; the Russians, though advancing through the Balkans, still had not taken Warsaw. The Allied air bombing had interrupted the German lines of communication and no more food parcels were arriving. We had a small reserve for a few months at half a parcel a week but that was hardly enough subsistence now that German rations were almost non-existent.

An extensive black market, organised by David Stirling and worked chiefly by Czecho, brought a certain amount of bread and eggs into the camp; Douglas Bader returned from his daily parole walks with his legs loaded with grain. This helped considerably but there were many hungry mouths to feed. The cold was intense and felt all the worse to our under-nourished bodies. The coal issued was very small and interminable arguments carried on as to whether we should try to warm all our bedrooms for a few hours of the day or make one common room really warm.

In order to keep sane I threw myself into activities which had never before interested me. For several months I helped Tony Rolt constructing a glider which after fourteen months' work was eventually completed around Christmas time. It was perhaps the most brilliant creation of the whole war in any prison camp. It was designed by a clever RAF officer called Goldfinch. Every single strut had to be sawed up and planed off from a floor board ripped up from one of the attics. These thousands of struts were nailed in place with boot nails. The metal work was made of our tin soup containers and the fabric from bed sheets.

It must seem incredible how a glider could remain concealed for fourteen months in a prison camp. One of the attics on the top floor was about eighty yards long. Material was collected and one Sunday afternoon a false wall was erected five yards from the end. The Germans inspected this attic daily but failed to notice that it was now only seventy-five yards long. They frequently tapped it but the false wall stood the test. It was entered through a trap door in the ceiling of the room below.

The glider held two people. It was to be launched by removing all the tiles from the roof after dark and attaching a very heavy weight to the end of a rope hooked on to a five yard runway. The roof was several hundred feet above the ground at this spot and experts judged that the risks were not much greater than launching a boat into the sea.

In view of the approaching end of the war, it was decided to keep the glider in case an officer had to be got away in an emergency. There was one such officer who was in a particularly precarious state. He was an American, Colonel Schaefer, who had been condemned to death for 'inciting mutiny' in his last camp. Actually he had been overheard telling someone to take no notice of a particularly stupid German order. He was kept in the cells and we always felt that his move could have been ordered at any time. Eventually he was the first man in the camp to be liberated and the glider was never used.

I took to reading philosophy, a subject about which I knew nothing and which soon absorbed me completely. Starting with Joad and Plato I worked up to Whitehead, who is, I suppose, the greatest philosopher of today. I found his writing hard to understand, but it opened up new vistas to the imagination and my brain turned somersaults in endeavouring to grasp his meaning and reach beyond to the ultimate problems of life. I used to discuss him for hours with Charlie Hopetoun who had read extensively and was completely obsessed with the subject.

It was a dangerous occupation for, living too much in the world of abstruse ideas, one lacked the outside occupations which bring one down to earth. As a diversion I took to acting and, after a short part in Shakespeare and a rather longer one as a wicked butler in a pantomime, I took part in J.B. Priestley's play *They Came to a City*. I enjoyed the rehearsals tremendously. The plays were put on with all the thoroughness of a West-End show. Only the best grease paint was used, carpenters and decorators worked for days on the stage and Teddy Barton was a tyrant in his own world. It was a valuable insight into a life of which I'd known nothing. Christmas came and went with a minimum of debauchery. Such great efforts had been put into it before, that this time we felt relieved to let it go quietly. The usual carols brought the usual nostalgic pain to our throats and a good dinner made us feel certain that this was indeed our last one in the bag.

We had several new members of our mess. Micky Burn was the first to join. In peace time he had been a foreign correspondent to *The Times* and was captured in the commando raid on St. Nazaire. He had a brilliant brain and a highly emotional temperament. His politics, very pink when he arrived, became redder as time went on. He discarded religion and became a Communist. The Russians were his gods who could do no wrong. It seems hard to think how he could have fitted into a mess like ours. I was personally very fond of him and found his conversation and arguments stimulating. He wrote good poetry which even T.S. Eliot admired and spent much time writing a book called *'And so Farewell'*, in which the characters were a clever mixture of those of our mess. The book was an allegory showing how the life and problems of prisoners were the reflection of humanity's problems crystallised into an intense form. Much of it was communist propaganda but very readable.

Giles Romilly, Lady Churchill's nephew, was another Communist who joined us. He was a moderate compared with Micky. He disapproved of Micky's theory that the Communist party was justified in getting and keeping in power by force. He was cleverer too. He wrote short stories which showed great insight into human nature and plays which were better than many I have seen in London. Redressing the political balance John Elphinstone, a cousin of the Queen, also joined us. He was a quiet thoroughly likeable character who never exposed his real feelings. He was a good influence in a mess which had extremes of feeling – Micky and Giles on the left and the two Charlies on the right.

Our political arguments used to last well into the night. The Charlies would get over-heated, especially Charlie Forrester who was blessed with few brains while John never showed emotion. Colin Mackenzie and I would balance on the fence, our birth and upbringing swaying us to the right, while our reasons drew us to the left. Martin would watch these arguments with a cynical smile. He was far too clever to become embroiled.

The ranks of the *prominenti* had become swollen as the war approached its climax. Besides John Elphinstone, two others arrived. George Lascelles, the King's nephew, was one of the youngest in the camp but remarkably old for his age. He had the manner and voice of his father and would argue black was white. One day I proved it:

'Good morning, George,' I said. 'Pretty cold to-day, isn't it'.
'Do you think so?' he answered. 'I thought it was much warmer.'
I tipped somebody else the wink and they went up to him.
'Good morning, George,' he said. 'Much warmer to-day, isn't it?'
'Do you think so?' said George looking genuinely surprised.
'I thought it was much colder'.

He was devoted to music and was well read for his age. He had been captured in Italy, where he was wounded accidently by one of his own patrol. I couldn't help feeling that prison was an invaluable experience for him!

Dawyck Haig, a son of Earl Haig, was a very different character, to whom I became very attached and I used to spend hours with him, reading and talking. Never was a son so unlike his father whom he criticised as a man of very narrow outlook. Dawyck was an extremely sensitive person. He was still groping for a philosophy of life and had by no means found his feet. His life was taken up with painting. He studied and practised it all day long. He had never been taught properly and his composition was full of faults. He tried to get me to criticise it but I knew so little that I found it impossible; I knew what I liked but had little further insight. 'That's no good at all,' Dawyck would say of my words, 'now if you had put that line there it would balance the other side, do you see? And that shade is all wrong. You want it light there and a bold dark line there. That will bring out the rest of the picture.' He was an unexpected person to be an art critic but he had been to the Slade and his criticisms were a revelation to me.

The Russian advances of the winter of 1944-5 were swifter and more devastating than ever. We began to see their effects at first hand. Orderly convoys of refugees passed through the village moving westwards; carts were piled high with their owners' belongings and, under the instructions of a commander, moved steadily with regular intervals between each cart. They brought with them stories of murder and rape claiming that the Russians were uncivilised barbarians. One such was that, on first entering a German house, a Russian soldier had found a lavatory. Suspicious of this queer looking contraption he fired a revolver into it; water spouted out whereupon the owner was shot for having a booby trap in her house. We did not believe these stories for we were enthusiastic admirers of our allies.

With the refugees came thousands of, mostly French, prisoners of war. They were marched for several hundred miles across the frozen country living on what food they could pick up on the way. Our camp was large enough to hold 500 PoWs but then contained about 400. One day we were told to crowd into a small wing of the castle in order to make room for 1,500 Frenchmen who were coming shortly. Their arrival marked the beginning of the last phase of our life in prison which was by far the toughest both physically and mentally. They streamed into the courtyard in a never ending crowd. Each man pushed a little trolley cart or a perambulator bearing his worldly possessions. They arrived filthy and lousy beyond belief but with irrepressible spirits as they argued, shouted and gesticulated with unimpaired vigour. They were thrust into every available corner of the camp, with only straw to lie on. With the cleanest crowd in the world conditions would have been deplorable, but with the French they were a nightmare. A stench pervaded the whole camp – a mixture of garlic, sweat and urine. The sound of their clogs on the cobbles and of their voices became a constant background to life.

From the moment they arrived our relations were vitiated by endless squabbles over food. The French view was that here we were, with at least six hundred parcels in the camp [enough for three more issues of half a parcel per man] in the best of health, while they were starving after their nightmare march. It seemed only right that we should share those parcels.

Colonel Tod took the exactly opposite line. He had seen, like so many of us, the well-packed suit cases of the French prisoners in 1940 and knew the incredible capacity the French had of carrying and keeping reserves of food. To dissipate our last reserves on this mob seemed criminal to him and his policy had our wholehearted approval. Relations deteriorated and the Black Market and squabbles over bartering increased the bad feeling. Yet despite this, the French kept up a veneer of good manners and one couldn't pass one on the stairs without him stopping and saying *'Pardon,'* to which we politely replied, *'Je vous en prie'*.

There were one or two of them with whom we made great friends and we gave them all the help possible in the way of food; one of these was Andre Haguet, a playwright many of whose works had been staged in pre-war Paris. We adopted him and he became our devoted admirer and went so far as to dedicate his latest play *Les Marionettes* to our mess.

Another friend was 'the butterfly man'. I don't think I ever knew his name, but his life work was in his collection, which he was proud to say was made entirely from butterflies caught behind the wire. They were beautifully laid out and our admiration of them gave him much pleasure. There was also another attractive chap called *'Le Philiponna'* who played the piano more beautifully than I have ever heard before or since. With two thousand people in the camp he had to keep very quiet about the time at which he played or he would have been crowded out. He had a partner who played the violin equally well, and I spent many afternoons completely carried away in the enjoyment of their concertos. The only piano in the camp was in the wash house. Into this we crowded, sat on a stool, shut our eyes and were wafted away from the squalor, hunger and fear that made up daily life and drifted into ecstasies of aesthetic enjoyment.

Professor Guitton was a very different man; he was a middle-aged philosopher from Montpellier with an extremely brilliant and agile brain. His arrival coincided with the climax of Charlie Hopetoun's philosophic studies when Charlie believed that he was on the verge of the greatest discovery of all time. Guitton and Haguet listened patiently to Charlie and showed enthusiasm for his views. This was the worst thing that could have happened. Gradually Charlie was overtaken by an obsession that he had the key to life, that he had solved all the problems of the world and that he was the greatest man alive. I do not know if Guitton was genuinely convinced or merely pandering to the eccentricities of the English aristocrats but the effect of this on us was devastating.

I had also been delving deeply into philosophy and but for the merest chance might have gone the same way as Charlie. The others in the mess saw the ludicrousness of the situation and we all tried to get Charlie to drop it but he became more and more intense. One afternoon he gave a lecture to about twenty 'intellectuals' in his room. Most of them had no idea what to expect. A few were completely taken in and became Charlie's disciples; the more I tried to persuade them of the folly of his arguments the angrier they became.

Charlie Forrester, whose brain went very little beyond horses, was infuriated with Charlie to no effect. Martin and David pursed their lips and kept out of his way. We were all feeling the mental strain which was made more acute by outside events. On the one hand our spirits were being raised by the news of the allied break through over the Rhine and the prospect of early liberation. Against that our bodies were getting weaker as the parcels had by now run out and we could not walk upstairs without dragging ourselves up by the bannisters and pausing on each landing. Our nerves were being tightened by the divergent pulls of anticipated liberation and the fear of starvation.

Then Charlie collapsed. At first it was a relief to have him out of the way and in bed; the onus of nursing him fell on Charlie Forrester, Pat Campbell-Preston and myself. The doctor, Hugh Dickie, was himself on the verge of a nervous break-down and would not go near Charlie. We were desperately worried as it was impossible to tell whether this was a nervous break-down or lunacy. It was unbearable to think that Charlie, the sanest person in the world who had done more than anyone else by his charm and brain and wit to keep us amused during the last five years, should lose his reason at the eleventh hour.

We took turns to nurse him; for hours he expounded his theories to me, quoting Whitehead, Plato and every known philosopher. For hours I would read to him to try and soothe his mind. He would have moments of lucidity and talk quite naturally and then suddenly an agonised look came over his face 'I'm sorry, Phil, but it's coming on again', he'd say and then put his hands to his face and burst into floods and floods of tears. I could hardly control myself or bear to see him in this condition.

This went on for about a week and every day brought the allied armies nearer. The imminent prospect of realizing five years' longing for 'the day' brought an unreality to every incident of life. Added to this was the fight for the very life of one of my best friends. It seemed like a race against time and I became obsessed with the need to bring Charlie back to sanity. All my will power was taken up with this effort.

Then came 12 April – the unique day within the last five years; like much of the rest of that week every incident stands out clearly in my memory. The Germans, conscious of their impending defeat, offered us a parole walk which was gladly accepted. A mixed party of many nationalities, including four or five from our mess, set out with only one German guard on our first excursion for a long while. It was a thrilling experience walking through the streets seeing the bread queues, shops and all the bright colours – sights of which we had been starved for so long.

From the town we went towards a large forest as the nominal object of the walk was to chop wood. We had for so long been cooped up within those stone walls that the simplest things gave us infinite pleasure – the green grass, the smell of a farmyard, the peasants in their country clothes. Arriving at a cross track in the forest, the German guard told us we could cut wood for the next four hours and be back there by 1500 hours. We all made off in different directions with our own mess forming one party.

It was an idyllic and utterly unreal day. Here was all the excitement and the novelty that Martin and I had felt when escaping but with the fear of discovery now replaced by the sound of heavy guns not so far off. We were told that there was a range nearby and attributed the noise to that; at the back of our minds we did wonder whether it might not be the Americans and, if so, what to do if they suddenly appeared. Did one's parole not to escape preclude one from being liberated? This was indeed a problem compounded by the awful thought of an American's scorn when he learnt that we were on parole; of course the noise must be from the range guns.

We chopped a good bit of wood and stacked it in a ride for a lorry to come and collect. We did not work hard for we were very weak and tired after the three mile walk. Once our consciences were eased by the wood we had chopped we set out in search of adventure. David and I soon came on a hut occupied by a Frenchman of whom we had learnt from a party who had been out the previous day. We sat down for a chat and presently produced a few packets of cigarettes. The Frenchman feigned surprise but shortly produced a dozen eggs and we returned to the rest of our mess feeling well pleased with ourselves.

We all moved on to look for a place for lunch and soon came upon a party of Poles working under a very tame Austrian. David engaged them in his newly learnt Russian with immediate success. One of them detached himself from the party, jumped on to a bicycle and disappeared while we settled ourselves down in a delightfully peaceful glade in the forest. Presently he reappeared on his bicycle with a sack on his handlebars. From this he produced a large quantity of sauerkraut, wrapped in a newspaper, potatoes, onions, beetroot and – best of all – bread.

We lit a fire, roasted the potatoes, boiled our eggs in a mess tin and settled down to a meal which I shall never forget. We had difficulty in making ourselves realize it was true. Here we were, apparently free, in the most beautiful forest, filling our aching stomachs with food to the heart's content.

We returned to our rendezvous at 1500 hours to find that two of the Frenchmen were still missing. We shouted for them for half an hour knowing well that they were probably in bed with some old frau miles away. This enraged us as parole was a sacred thing which must never be violated. Almost more annoying was the sight of two Frenchmen with the most enormous bundles of potatoes on their backs inadequately hidden under a greatcoat. We had taken great pains to distribute our few eggs, potatoes and bread judiciously between us, but now we were in danger of getting the whole party searched and discredited.

There was nothing for it but to try and conceal them as best we could. With difficulty they staggered back to Colditz where the sentry at the gate arrested them but, to our great relief, allowed the rest of us to pass without being searched. No sooner were we in the camp than we were greeted by the news of staggering advances. The Americans, it appeared, were now within twenty kilometres of Chemnitz and Leipzig. Leipzig was due north of us and Chemnitz to the south-east. Without doubt it was the Americans' guns that we had heard.

That evening, John Winant, the son of the American Ambassador to England, was ordered by the Germans to pack up his things and proceed into the Commandantür. We sat down to supper in a strained atmosphere. Giles Romilly and John Elphinstone were both convinced that John's removal was merely a prelude to the removal of all the *prominenti* from the camp. There was every reason to believe this and we questioned if they should go into hiding. Hiding meant acute discomfort for several days and perhaps weeks with every chance of discovery by the Germans who would leave no stone unturned. No decision was reached that evening.

At 2230 hours, after the lights were out and we were all confined to our rooms, the Germans marched into the courtyard in strength, posted a sentry on all doors and ordered all the remaining *prominenti*, who were intended to be used as hostages, to move at once. We all waited and watched anxiously until about midnight when a sorry procession filed across the yard to the main gate – John Elphinstone, George Lascelles, Dawyck Haig, Michael Alexander, Giles Romilly, and finally Charlie. They were followed by General Bor Komorovsky and the Poles who were on his staff in the Warsaw rising. We shouted 'Goodbye' but our feelings were of utter impotence. We had stood by and watched our friends being led away without raising a finger to help them. God only knew whether we should see any of them again and the fate of Charlie did not bear contemplating.

It eventually transpired that there was a clear Nazi intention to use them as hostages; they were moved westward towards Bavaria in the custody of a number of different high ranking officers before John finally prevailed on a German General to hand them over to the advancing Americans. A few weeks later he showed me the pearl studded revolver which his captor had given him as a souvenir! They suffered no casualties and Charlie made a complete recovery.

It was with heavy hearts that we woke up next day. By now there was no mistaking the sound of gunfire which was shaking the very window frames. The wireless was being manned twelve hours a day and those of us who had helped to 'stooge' during the nightly news services of the past months were allowed up for the first time to listen.

Although I had been 'stooging' for about five months I still did not know how or where it was hidden. Three of us filed up into the attic, picked the lock of a grid-iron door which led into the very roof top and carefully crossed the floor covering our footsteps with dust. Dick Howe, who was in charge of the wireless, stopped at one of the floor boards and pulled out a small bit of wood, slid the board an inch to the right and it was raised.

We let ourselves down into the gap while the board was replaced over our heads; in pitch darkness we crawled along between the boards to the eaves of the roof. There we turned left to face another wall and Dick repeated the operation on one of its boards, removed it and we clambered through the gap into a small apartment. He switched on an electric light and replaced the board.

It was a brilliantly constructed hide and reminded me at once of the cockpit of an aeroplane. There were two stools and a desk. On the desk was a large sheet of blotting paper, some writing pads and pencils and two pairs of ear phones. On the walls were maps of all the fronts, with the latest lines marked in red. In the centre was the wireless-set above which were red and green lights. These were the 'danger' and 'all clear' signals in case a German came up into the attic.

If by a miracle the Germans had actually come upon the hide while the news was being taken, they would still not have caught either the wireless-set or the occupants. For there was a trap door through which they would have descended together with part of the ceiling on to the heads of the astonished people in the room below.

We listened to the news from America, Britain, Germany, Holland and France. Dick was continually scribbling notes in fluent shorthand. He was a versatile chap. Besides being an excellent wireless operator he was a good linguist, shorthand writer and no mean craftsman. For three years he had run the escape committee with remarkable success. No better man could have done this job. We heard the voice of the British announcer and the sound of Big Ben. I felt the voice of civilisation reaching right through to us as if an invisible hand had been stretched out from England. We were in touch with what had seemed unattainable for so long.

Chapter 12

Liberation

The next day, 14 April, we were roused early by Colonel Tod himself, who came round to each room and said: 'Prepare to move by 10 o'clock. I shall do what I can to stop the move, but it may not be possible.' This news fell on us like a sledgehammer. Our innermost fears had been realised. Liberation had always seemed a dream which might happen to others but would never happen to us. We were a *Sonderlager*. Despite the departure of the *prominenti* the camp was still full of people whom the Germans were particularly anxious to guard and keep guarded. We had known in our heart of hearts that this would happen and now we were off for a march into Bavaria where, from his stronghold, Hitler would barter our lives against his own.

We packed our few belongings and waited, while a momentous interview went on in the *Commandantür*. Tod arrived with Martin who had been his adjutant for the last year and Lance Pope, his interpreter. As he arrived a Colonel of the SS left the Commandant's office and waited next door. The interview opened with Prawitt, the commandant, icily cold and collected as usual, while Eggers the security officer, stood beside him smirking nervously. Eggers was the most dangerous German in the camp – a self-professed Anglophobe he loathed us with the hatred of a clever man whose son had been killed by us and who saw his own race being beaten by a better side.

'You will be ready to move by 10 o'clock,' said Prawitt. So did a conference open which was to last for three hours. At the end of it Tod had used his diplomacy to the full and Prawitt had capitulated. A 'gentleman's agreement' was reached by both sides. Prawitt gave his word that nobody should be moved from the camp and that not a shot would be fired against the Americans by a single German under his command. Tod gave his word that the British would not take over the camp from the Germans by force and he gave Prawitt a certificate stating that he had behaved correctly. Prawitt retained the attitude of a dignified Prussian officer to the end, but Eggers broke down in the middle of the meeting and, after a snivelling whining plea for the safety of his wife, he left the room.

The news was greeted in the camp with inexpressible relief and Tod's prestige, already high among all nationalities, was now supreme. That evening an air raid siren was heard blowing short blasts which denoted that allied tank spearheads were in the neighbourhood. We crowded the windows, but all we could see was feverish activity on the hill sides, where Germans of the 'Home Guard' were digging emplacements, and a small party down by the bridge where an explosive charge was being laid. Their efforts looked uncoordinated and amateurish – like schoolboys on a 'Field Day'.

Next day, Sunday 15 April, we went to church. Padre Heard had just started his sermon when there was a drone outside. It sounded very different from the ordinary heavy bombers which came over in formation every day. An American plane flashed past the window and its roar was followed by the stutter of machine gun fire.

We sat in our chairs as only a British congregation would sit while Heard finished his sermon in his own time. Once out of the room, we rushed to the windows. American Typhoons and Mustangs were circling around Colditz looking for targets. One by one they would dive, pour out a stream of tracer bullets and rise into the air again. There was no opposition. A German truck was driving up the road on the far side of the town and was spotted by the American plane. As it dived the lorry lurched into the ditch and the crew bailed out. A burst of fire set the lorry blazing. It was a glorious spectacle.

Meanwhile the noise of the gunfire came nearer and nearer from the wood on the hill overlooking the town. Suddenly we observed several dark objects appear and start manoeuvring on the outskirts of the wood. Were they enemy or allied tanks?

The question was soon answered as a flash and a roar was followed by a cloud of smoke appearing from a collapsed house on the outskirts of the town. One by one the houses which we had stared at for year after year and, which we had come to know and to hate, collapsed in a pile of smoke until the outskirts of the town were ringed by blazing fires and smoke. I watched from the fourth floor of the Saalhouse – the senior officers' block – and felt like a spectator at a play. It never occurred to me that those shells, which were landing half a mile away, might next be directed at our castle. It was an unforgettable spectacle.

Our sense of security was broken by a shattering crash. Something had undoubtedly landed somewhere very close and the staircase was crowded, as people rushed to the ground floor. I met Peter Dollar blinking short-sightedly.

'What's happened to your spectacles?' I asked him.

'Blown off my bloody nose,' said Peter. 'The shell came right through the wall of the room we were in. Lucky it was only AP [anti-personnel] or we'd have had it. As it was Douglas Bader was sent for six and had to get out on his hands and knees.'

I left the Saalhouse and went back to our mess room which was also on the fourth floor. They had heard the crash but didn't realise a shell had hit the castle. We watched for a while as the battle enveloped more and more of the town. Shells were falling up to the foot of the castle. Never again as long as we lived should we witness such a scene. Here, perched high up above the town and the surrounding country, we had the most perfect view of a modern battle.

The Germans were putting up a lively fight and seemed bent on holding the line of the river running through the town. Unfortunately we were on the far side of the river and it seemed as if the key to its defence must be the castle itself. The Americans realised this and, as we later learnt, brought up all their artillery to smash the castle to bits. The gun position officer had finished ranging on the castle and was about to give the order to fire when someone noticed a little union jack flying from one of the windows. This undoubtedly saved the lives of many hundreds of us. The gunner told us afterwards that not many stones of Colditz would have been left standing. The flags had been carefully made months before with little thought to the vital use to which they would be put.

Meanwhile the Germans decided it was time to pull back over the river and blow the bridge. After the last man was over there was a pause and we could see one or two men running to and fro. Suddenly there was a dull explosion. Stones and debris flew into the air. When they subsided we saw that there was a crater in a few feet of the pavement but the bridge was otherwise quite undamaged. The attempt looked ludicrous and we gave a loud cheer of derision.

The American tanks and guns were now closing in on the town and shells were falling fast and furious all round us. The order was given to everybody to crowd down into the basement and the ground floor into pre-arranged positions. The rest of that day I spent in the small room which had once been Charlie Hopetoun's bedroom. The very thick walls made it feel fairly secure. We had left the majority of our belongings packed up and brought only food and blankets with us.

From time to time rumours came flying in. A shell had fallen in the *Commandantür*, next door to where the Commandant's wife was taking refuge. The Americans had crossed the river above and below the town. The Germans in the camp had asked us to put out more flags. There was a German armoured division in the neighbourhood. If they decided to make a final stand here we would be moved into the woods.

The German sentries were behaving with admirable correctness. They no longer manned the high watch towers but wandered aimlessly round the castle taking cover now and again as a shell whined towards and over them. I looked out of a small window facing the rear of the castle. As I watched there was a whine and a shriek; a tree crashed and a shell exploded only twenty yards away. I flattened myself on the floor and, when I looked up I saw the charred crater and the splintered trunk of the tree. From the same direction came the splutter of machine gun fire. It sounded as if the Americans were behind us now and the garrison surrounded.

As it grew dark, we began to settle ourselves down for the night. There was no more machine gun fire but shells whined ceaselessly overhead. Presently Stephen Wright appeared dramatically in the doorway, gazed round the room and made for me.

'Have you heard the plan?' he asked.
'What plan?'
'A party of us are going to escape through to the American lines and tell them about the *prominenti* and try to get a force sent

through to rescue them straight away. David Stirling is coming and Micky Burn. Why don't you come too?'

The futility of such a scheme would not have impressed a child. No-one knew where the *prominenti* were and the Americans were hardly likely to launch a force into the blue on such a wild goose chase. Anyway we should be able to tell them all about it tomorrow. I told him I was not coming. I could imagine him and Micky going but, if David went too, it would be for a different reason. In fact the expedition never materialised.

We had a restless night. Shells whined overhead all the time and I kept waiting semi-conscious for the crash of one hitting the castle. We woke up to find peace and quiet reigning. The silence was uncanny. One of two things must have happened – either the Americans had abandoned the attack or the Germans had withdrawn under cover of darkness.

We went up to our room on the fourth floor. The town was a sea of white flags, blankets, sheets, handkerchiefs and table cloths fluttering from every window. And still we doubted. Where were the Americans? Why did the castle gates remain locked?

We strained our eyes as far as the street parallel to the river and up to the bridge. There we could make out a small party of men – perhaps half a dozen – moving methodically from one house to another. Surely they must be Americans and yet why were there so few of them? They reached the bridge and stopped. As we watched, we saw someone walking across the bridge. There was a shout, followed by the splutter of a tommy gun, and the man sprawled forward and lay kicking in the middle of the road. So it was the Americans.

Our hearts leapt into our mouths, our spirits surged high up and we became intoxicated by the relief and excitement, the realisation that at any moment now we would be free. Free! Free! Free! It seemed impossible. The endless monotony, the barbed wire, the stone walls, the iron bars – all these were over. Our hunger, our weakness, our petty squabbles, our eccentricities and inhibitions – all were forgotten as the great truth surged up and hit us with its full force.

The gate of the courtyard opened and a dark, dust-begrimed, weary GI walked in. Immediately he was overwhelmed by a crowd of two thousand hysterically cheering officers, yelling themselves hoarse, crying even. Those nearest him embraced him, kissed him on both cheeks. He had to fight to keep his feet, and still his weary eyes gazed automatically up at the walls and windows searching for a hostile rifle – part of the training required in the many towns he had liberated in the past few weeks.

More Americans followed him. They all bore the same look. They were obviously suffering from several days' lack of sleep, covered in dust and grime, hard as nails, with that look of self-sufficiency that had saved them their lives.

We were all affected differently. The French were hysterical. Many of the British, true to form, hid their feelings. They were ashamed to behave otherwise. Pat, who had been cooking some porridge for breakfast, stolidly went on cooking. Colonel Schaefer, who had spent months in solitary confinement under sentence of death, was already wearing his tin hat and had a revolver strapped to his belt. Many others had acquired revolvers miraculously from somewhere or other. The Americans told us they had suffered more casualties in the Battle of Colditz than anywhere since the Battle of the Rhine. The Hitler Youth had given them the most trouble. A party of thirty Americans had been ambushed and suffered very heavily. Many of these Germans were schoolboys who would lie down on their own doorsteps and fire their guns until blown to bits. Devils they were, and tragic as one thought of the purpose such zeal might have been used.

Meanwhile the German guard company had been lined up in the courtyard outside. An American went methodically down the line frisking them of their watches, rings and other articles of value. Prawitt standing dignified at the end of the row was subjected to the same treatment. He objected, produced Tod's certificate, and pointed out that he was the commandant of Colditz – all to no avail. Through jeering, booing crowds they were marched off to a life which would have held few illusions.

When we heard that they had been 'frisked' we were indignant because, for all their faults, the Germans had respected our property. When I was captured, I was given a receipt for £6.7s.8d. This money had followed me through five years and seven camps and, a week before our release, it was handed back to me. We would have liked to see our captors treated fairly but we had little say in the matter.

At first everybody was confined to the camp unless on duty. I had been given the job together with Peter Dollar, Charlie Forrester and one or two others of taking over the horse transport in the town and bringing rations into the camp on the carts. We went down to look at the stables. Passing through the town we saw much broken glass and a few gutted houses but not many. Most of the damage was on the outskirts. There were about a dozen horses and half a dozen carts in the stables. We wandered around like children given a new toy to play with. We talked to some Ukrainian girls who had been deported from their country and made to work in Colditz. They lived just below the castle and the sound of their nostalgic songs used to reach us in the camp.

There had been a camp of Jews in the town about which we had heard little but rumours. These people, who had been imprisoned and brutally starved for up to ten years, had stayed alive only for the hope of this day. Two days before our liberation, however, the Germans had lined them up against a wall and mown them down with machine guns. Only one survived by falling down and pretending he was dead. He dragged himself up to the camp – a pitiful wreck. His arms and legs were like match-sticks, his face sunken and there were hollows beneath his eyes into which a golf ball could have fitted. No wonder that the Americans had little time to spare for the Germans.

That night one of the Americans – Burrows by name – came and dined with us. We had a big meal, finishing up our parcels and helping them down with some wine. We listened open-mouthed to the stories he had to tell. Although only a private soldier, a signaller in fact, he had all the *savoir faire* and education of an officer.

Next morning Charlie and I were up with the lark. We had a hot shower, got onto our bicycles and away to the horse transport lines to muck out and get the stables done. We came back with a tremendous appetite and sat down to a breakfast of three fresh scrambled eggs, bacon and all the other luxuries of an English breakfast. Then back we went to get the rations up and carry out various jobs around the place. I was never an expert in a trap but these cart horses were more than a handful. There was a very bad moment as I was trying to thread my way through a mass of vehicles, when the horses bolted and overturned a huge cooker with the Americans' dinners on board.

The *Gauleiter* of Colditz was the worst type of Nazi and, as Peter Dollar knew where his house was, he sent me round to see if I could fetch him. I took Burrows with me, as I liked the look of his Sten Gun. We knocked on the door which was opened by our objective's wife. She said her husband had left a few days before so we asked to look around her house. On the first floor she showed us into a room where the shelves were literally stacked with the best wines in Europe. Champagne, brandy, burgundy, claret, hock, mosello there they all stood and very good vintages too, doubtless looted from France in 1940.

I had no hesitation where my duty lay. She provided me with a sack, and helped me make my selection. She appeared quite relieved to get rid of the wine on to me, rather than on to some Americans who would get drunk and smash up the house. I reported my find to Peter Dollar, who sent me straight back with Jack Pringle and this time we really took our time in selecting the pick of a very large bunch.

Heavily laden I staggered back to the camp up to my mess, who were preparing the biggest dinner that had ever been seen, consisting largely of pork which the Americans had brought into the camp in large quantities. That night we stayed over our dinner for many a long hour and consumed considerably more than a bottle per head. When at last Charlie and I staggered down to our room we only got ourselves into bed with the greatest difficulty. A precarious period, spent trying to avoid rolling off, was followed by pangs of pain in my stomach which had not known fresh meat, let alone pork, for many a day. My head began to protest against the quantity and variety of the drink and never in my life have I had such a night. To make matters worse the Germans who, we later learnt were only a thousand yards away, started shelling the town. I had nightmares of a counter-attack and the recapture of Colditz. I pictured an identity parade with us all lined up while the wife of the *Gauleiter* moved slowly down the ranks until she stopped and picked on me. What followed was so terrible that it woke me up but further nightmares followed. Early next morning the door burst open and our bumptious Brigadier bounced in looking hale and hearty. 'Have you heard the news?' he cried. 'We leave at 8 o'clock. Home to-morrow. Top hole, what!' 'Get out,' I groaned. 'I don't want to go home.'

Somehow we got dressed in time. With our few valuables in a suitcase or kit bag, we stood waiting in the courtyard. It still seemed impossible that we were really going home. I felt too ill to care but everybody else seemed to have quickly acquired some article of loot – shot guns, rifles, cameras or field-glasses.

After a two-hour wait, the word came at last – to move, and we marched out of the camp for the last time, down the alley way, through the *Commandant□r* over the moat and into the town. Never again would I see that castle.

There was further delay in the town and only later did we learn the reason. The front line was still only a thousand yards away and, behind that, many parties of Germans remained to be mopped up. That very morning, in a wood through which we had to pass, an American lorry had been ambushed. The local commander, Colonel Shaughnessy, was still waiting for reports that it was clear.

At last he was satisfied. We climbed into our lorries and began our journey home. It was a nightmare drive. Looking around we saw the contrast of exuberantly happy faces and some, like myself, a deathly green. Martin looked awful, David Stirling worse and both Pat and David Walker pretty bad. Passing through a wood the leading lorry stopped abruptly. The remainder of the convoy halted and tried to turn. A knocked-out enemy tank-buster had been spotted through the trees and they were taking no chances. At about mid-day, we saw a whole battery of guns deployed in a ploughed field. The convoy stopped and, to our surprise, the battery opened fire on a little copse a hundred yards from the road along which we had just passed. Another party of Germans was being encouraged to surrender and we hated to think how closely we had driven to them.

We had a bite of lunch while we waited and soon became aware of the most pungent odour. Just as I was forcing some spam down my throat I noticed bloated German corpses. To this day I cannot eat spam without thinking of that smell.

We drove on through the shattered town of Naumburg and over rolling country past battle-knocked-out vehicles, crashed aeroplanes and wrecked houses. As it was growing dark we arrived at the aerodrome of Colleda. I looked for a doctor, swallowed several pills of aspirin, opium and M and B and passed quietly out.

Next day I woke up feeling a new man. Fortified by American rations we marched out to the airfield still unable to believe that the aeroplanes would really turn up. They did and we filed into the hard seats of the Dakotas and away up into the air over the flames of Germany, over the Rhine, over Calais, over the Channel and, at last, over the green fields of England and outskirts of London before we came slowly down to Bovingdon.

Twenty-four hours later I was met by my family on Kemble station.